Communication Plus

Florence and Marita are two of the most effective communicators
in our country. Who better to write *Communication Plus*? I've listened
to them both and I've never been sorry.

PATSY CLAIRMONT
PUBLIC SPEAKER AND BEST-SELLING AUTHOR

Florence and Marita are two of my most favorite people. Everyone should
read the words written by this mother-daughter team . . . your life
and heart will be forever challenged and changed.

EMILIE BARNES
PUBLIC SPEAKER AND AUTHOR
FOUNDER, MORE HOURS IN MY DAY MINISTRIES

The Littauers and their superb teaching on communication is
the foundation on which many of us who are leaders stand! Both Bill
and I are grateful for the practical training, wisdom and equipping we
gained through CLASS and our relationship with the Littauers! Now it
is in book form! Awesome! Every person seeking to influence should
have a copy of *Communication Plus* on his or her shelf.

PAM AND BILL FARREL
AUTHOR, *MEN ARE LIKE WAFFLES, WOMEN ARE LIKE SPAGHETTI*
AND *10 BEST DECISIONS A PARENT CAN MAKE*

Communication Plus, by seasoned speakers and mentors Florence
and Marita Littauer, is a step-by-step guide to everything you need to
become a professional speaker--from preparing your program to dressing
for the platform--and everything in between. Here is a one-stop excursion
into the world of professional speaking for Christians who want to bring
hope and help to a hurting world. The authors' practical wisdom
and their hearts for God shine through each page.

KAREN O'CONNOR
SPEAKER AND AUTHOR
HELP, LORD! I'M HAVING A SENIOR MOMENT AND
SQUEEZE THE MOMENT: MAKING THE MOST OF LIFE'S GIFTS AND CHALLENGES

We tend to think that if we can talk, we can communicate. Florence and Marita convince us otherwise in this classic, insightful text that turns "talk" into real communication. Once you finish this book, you will not only be heard, but your message will also be understood.

JILL RIGBY

CEO, MANNERS OF THE HEART COMMUNITY FUND
AUTHOR, *RAISING RESPECTFUL CHILDREN IN A DISRESPECTFUL WORLD*
AND *THE BUSINESS OF MANNERS*

This practical, readable book is jam-packed with ideas that will transform your ability to communicate—personally and professionally, in person and on paper.

GLENNA SALSBURY

PUBLIC SPEAKER AND AUTHOR
PAST PRESIDENT, NATIONAL SPEAKERS ASSOCIATION

Many books promise to change your life, but this one will enable you to do more: to change *other people's lives* for the better. Read it, live it, and change your world!

DONNA PARTOW

PUBLIC SPEAKER AND BEST-SELLING AUTHOR

MARITA LITTAUER
FLORENCE LITTAUER

Best-Selling Author of *Personality Plus*

Regal

PUBLISHED BY REGAL BOOKS
FROM GOSPEL LIGHT
VENTURA, CALIFORNIA, U.S.A.
PRINTED IN THE U.S.A.

Regal Books is a ministry of Gospel Light, a Christian publisher dedicated to serving the local church. We believe God's vision for Gospel Light is to provide church leaders with biblical, user-friendly materials that will help them evangelize, disciple and minister to children, youth and families.

It is our prayer that this Regal book will help you discover biblical truth for your own life and help you meet the needs of others. May God richly bless you.

For a free catalog of resources from Regal Books/Gospel Light, please call your Christian supplier or contact us at 1-800-4-GOSPEL or www.regalbooks.com.

Library of Congress Cataloging-in-Publication Data
Littauer, Florence, 1928-
  Communication plus / Florence and Marita Littauer.
    p. cm.
  ISBN 0-8307-3931-9 (trade paper)
  1. Oral communication. I. Littauer, Marita. II. Title.
  P95.L576 2006
  302.2'242—dc22   2006008656

1   2   3   4   5   6   7   8   9   10   /   10   09   08   07   06

Rights for publishing this book in other languages are contracted by Gospel Light Worldwide, the international nonprofit ministry of Gospel Light. Gospel Light Worldwide also provides publishing and technical assistance to international publishers dedicated to producing Sunday School and Vacation Bible School curricula and books in the languages of the world. For additional information, visit www.gospellightworldwide.org; write to Gospel Light Worldwide, P.O. Box 3875, Ventura, CA 93006; or send an e-mail to info@gospellightworldwide.org.

Contents

Preface

FLORENCE LITTAUER

• •

From the time I was a child, I wanted to be a teacher. I would line up my dolls and teach them nursery rhymes. I took elocution lessons and performed confidently at the recitals. I taught ballroom dancing in a friend's garage using an old, rejected wind-up Victrola for the music and followed those charts in magazines with little footprints directing which way to make one's feet go. All this while I never could get a grip on the waltz myself!

When I was in college, I taught drama at a summer camp. One day, the archery teacher quit. The job was offered up for an extra $100, and since I needed the money, I took the job. I did a quick study of the manual and began to teach the children how to stand and shoot—even though I could never hit the target myself. When a child would ask me to demonstrate my shooting skills, I would say, "Your parents did not pay big money for you to watch me perform. They paid for me to teach you how to become a little Robin Hood." This clear answer seemed logical, and the children soon stopped asking me to show my talents. Experiences such as these taught me that I could teach things that I did not necessarily know how to do myself.

Once I received my degree, I taught speech on the high school and college levels. As soon as I became a Christian, I also began to teach Bible studies. My approach was considered fresh and applicable. As one lady remarked, I was "unencumbered by theological training." I added humor to my messages; in fact, when I asked my mother what she thought of my teaching, she replied, "They do seem to find you amusing." With those words of encouragement, I moved ahead with my speaking career.

By the time I became more than "amusing," I realized that there were few gifted women speakers in the Christian market. Some had stories to tell, but they didn't quite know how to tell them. Some were so deep in the Word that few of the folks in their audiences could really understand what they were teaching. I thought that perhaps my education and experience could help these talented women get their message across more effectively.

In the fall of 1980, I felt led to put together an invitation-only seminar for those who desired to improve their communication skills. I had been teaching a Bible study in Hollywood, and four of these ladies—Rhonda Flemming, Joanne Dru, Jeanne Cagney and Bonnie Green—were eager to come. They all came out to Redlands for our speaker training seminar, along with Patsy Clairmont, Emilie Barnes and my two daughters. In January 1981, we had our first training of 43 women. We worked together from 9:00 in the morning until 9:00 at night for four days—and wrapped things up with a shopping trip to Los Angeles to buy clothes appropriate for Christian speakers.

I had only intended to do this seminar once, but Patsy asked if we could hold another one in Detroit. The Hollywood ladies put on one there, and then a group in Texas planned the first big speaker training seminar—one that required staff. Next came a seminar at the Crystal Cathedral, and we moved on from there. This year, 2006, is our twenty-fifth anniversary.

Marita Littauer

· ·

I would have never predicted from our simple beginnings in a bank building in Redlands, California, that today we would be celebrating 25 years of Christian service. When my mother and I organized our first speaker training seminar—back before it became the CLASSeminar—we had no idea what doors God would open or where walking through those doors would take us. We simply followed the path as He directed our steps.

As we traveled throughout the country speaking together, the event planners would frequently ask my mother, "Do you know any good speakers?" Back then there was no single resource to which a meeting planner could go to find speakers—no Internet to search. It was all by word of mouth. We had met many women who had a marvelous message, but they needed help in communicating it effectively. There were others who had great stage presence, but they were scared to be up front or had no confidence that they had anything to say. The combination of these two needs—event planners needing good speakers and speakers needing focus and refinement—precipitated that first gathering 25 years ago. My mother, Florence, did all the teaching, while I figured out where we'd go to lunch and created handouts as she developed the next teaching material. From her background as an English and speech teacher, her giftings as a speaker, and her time on the platform, she taught the women the practical methods and proven plans they needed to communicate with confidence.

As we seemed to be meeting a need, we determined that this training needed a name. I remember sketching out names and rough drafts of a logo during a flight. I came up with the name CLASS, which stood for "Christian Leaders And Speakers Seminar." The name stuck. As we began to receive invitations to offer CLASS throughout the country, we built a team that could lead the small groups and share in the teaching.

We engaged in some expansion as additional needs were expressed. First, we added the Speaker Services department. Again, we never planned to add a "department," we just walked through the doors as God opened them. Through what had become the CLASS offices, we began coordinating the Christian Leaders And Speakers Seminars and Florence's ever-increasing speaking schedule. Because of the seminars, we had now trained hundreds of people—including men—and had a core staff that made up our teaching team.

The seminars grew right along at the rate of Florence's speaking invitations. Often when someone called our office looking for Florence, she was already booked or was outside their budget range. Whoever took the call would hear a desperate voice on the other end of the phone plead, "Do you know anyone else I could find to speak for us?" Since we had a teaching staff of excellent speakers and a cadre of trained speakers, we started recommending them. Once we offered options to these needy meeting planners, they began asking for speakers who could address specific topics. So we'd search our collective memory for people who had attended CLASS, looking for a match. This process of matching the groups in need of a speaker with the CLASS graduates who were ready and available is what we now call Speaker Services, which represents more than 200 men and women nationwide.

Around that same time, I remember my father calling me into his office. He declared, "Your mother's publishers are obviously not doing anything to help her get 'out there.' " I wholeheartedly agreed with his assessment. He then added, "We are going to have to do that ourselves." I nodded in agreement. "That is your new job," he then said.

In a back office, we had a couple of old directories from the National Religious Broadcasters Association. I grabbed my mother's speaking schedule and looked up radio stations in the cities where she'd be visiting. I called the station managers and told them that Florence would be available for interviews when she was in the area. Since the radio stations had local programming needs that had to be filled, they were typically thrilled that I'd called. As I became acquainted with the talk-show hosts, they began to ask if I knew anyone else who would like to be on their show. Many of my friends were authors, so I would suggest them to the hosts.

Several of my author friends had been published by the same publisher as my mother. This publisher began to notice an increase in sales based on the radio interviews that I had set up for my friends. One day, I received a call from this publisher to ask if I could do this for all their authors. Before long, CLASS was retained by many of the major publishers in the industry—as well as individual authors—and the CLASS Promotional Service was born. To date, thousands of interviews with authors have been booked on both radio and television as a result of the efforts of CLASS Promotional Services.

Around 1993, we began to see a shift in the industry. The publishing world was noticing a difference in book sales when the author was also a speaker. As a result, publishers now wanted their authors to also be speakers. To meet this new demand, we adjusted the CLASSeminar's content to include an introduction on "turning your message into a book" and changed our name to reflect this addition. CLASS now stood for the "Christian Leaders, Authors and Speakers Seminar."

Because we were now producing popular speakers whose audience members were asking for their books, it soon became clear that we needed to use our connections in Christian publishing to help them get published. (By 1992, I'd written five books and my mother had written more than you could count on your fingers.) To facilitate this connection, in 1995 we added what we called the CLASS Reunion—an event held in conjunction with the annual Christian Booksellers Association's international trade show. It was designed to connect our CLASS graduates with publishers who were looking for speakers to publish. For two days, in brief face-to-face meetings, attendees could share their ideas with the publishers' representatives, and the editors could express whether the idea was something that fit their needs. The CLASS Reunion also gave attendees the opportunity to walk the floor of the closed-to-the-public trade show. As those who attended the CLASS Reunion seminars spread the word about their resulting publishing success, the seminars quickly became sold-out events. Attendees soon learned that they really needed to attend twice—once to learn how the industry works, and the second time to come ready with a proposal or manuscript in hand.

The CLASS Reunion was strictly about connections and did not offer any specific training. However, by 2001 it became clear to us that something was needed to bridge the gap between the CLASSeminar and the CLASS Reunion. While there were many terrific writers' conferences around the country, there was nothing to help speakers make the move from being a speaker to getting published. In January 2002, we launched the CLASS Career Coaching Conference, which combined a mini-Class Reunion-style event with training in both speaking refinement and getting published. Once aspiring authors completed the CLASSeminar and the CLASS Career Coaching Conference (now called Advanced CLASS) and had an active speaking ministry, they were virtually assured publishing success at the CLASS Reunion (now called Publishing Connections Conference).

One of those terrific writers' conferences was the Glorieta Christian Writers Conference, held each year in Glorieta, New Mexico, at the LifeWay Glorieta Conference Center. Because I live in New Mexico, I had frequently been invited to teach at this writers' conference. In October 2001, the former director resigned. The thought of taking over the leadership of this great conference kept nagging at me in the back of my mind, and in January 2002, I could no longer ignore its pull. I contacted LifeWay and found that a new director had not yet been chosen. Within two weeks, CLASS and LifeWay had signed an agreement to create what has since become a friendly and favorable partnership. In the past four years, the Glorieta Christian Writers' Conference has virtually doubled in size. It now has more than 350 attendees, 100 faculty members and several media representatives—a total of nearly 500 people.

It gives me great joy to look back over the last 25 years and see the Lord's guidance and direction for my life. The seminar that my mother started back in 1981 has grown into a Christian ministry—a full-service agency providing resources, training and promotion for both established and aspiring Christian speakers, authors and publishers.

We hope that this book will encourage you to continue your own training as you prepare yourself for the plans God has in mind for you. When He opens a door, walk through it. You'll enjoy the trip!

CHAPTER 1

Figuring Out What You Have to Say

FLORENCE LITTAUER

. . . .

Frequently, after I've spoken at a luncheon or retreat, a lady will come up to me and say, "I want to be a speaker like you." Of course, what she really means is, "It looks fun and easy up there on the platform. I think I could do that." I'm grateful that a message that I've spent years composing, polishing and perfecting still comes across as fresh and new. I want my message to simply roll off my tongue—smoothly and effortlessly. I want it to appear as if it just came to my mind as I stood there. In fact, many of my best lines do seem to come out of nowhere. But I know that while I'm speaking, the Lord can give me new material more easily if I'm confident enough in my message to relax enough to hear Him.

So where do we start? Let's pretend you're asking me how to be a speaker. I ask, "What do you have to say?" You will probably reply, "Well, I could talk about . . ." to which I will respond, "No, no. We don't talk about *things*; we have something to say."

What do *you* have to say? What do you have to say that is so exciting you can't keep quiet about it? What corner of life have you explored that I have not gone to? What has the Lord done for you that I haven't yet experienced? What do *you* have to say?

Ideas should start jumping around in your head. You should be saying, "I've always wanted to share that . . ." or "There's a great lesson in this part of my life" or "People could learn from this." Once subject ideas begin to come to you, I would then ask if anyone needs to hear your message. Could God use your words to change a person's life? Or is what you have to say so specific to your own situation that it wouldn't fit anyone else's needs?

Pertinence and Preparation

I once had the opportunity to speak at a business convention in Australia. After the session, a young man came up to me and said, "I'd like to be a speaker like you."

"What do you have to say?" I replied.

"Well, I could talk about what I do."

"What do you do?"

"I sell used toys at flea markets."

Now, even assuming that this man knows more about used toys than anyone else in the world, how many people in a given audience would want to hear about it?

Conversely, there are many people who do have a life-changing message to share with the world. One such individual was Doug, whom Marita met on an airplane. As they chatted about our ministry during the flight, Doug got excited. He was interested in speaking. He had done public speaking as a part of his profession, but he felt that his words had lost a sense of purpose.

Doug had been the victim of sexual abuse. He told Marita, "Through therapy and spiritual guidance, I now feel that I am being called to share something that is important for the world to hear—especially for men and women who have also experienced sexual abuse." With sexual abuse being such a widespread problem, Doug certainly has something to say that people need to hear—especially since it is coming from a male perspective. Marita encouraged Doug to keep track of the changes in his life as he worked through his own issues in therapy and moved toward sharing his life.

I once had a pastor who was an excellent and charming Bible teacher when he was prepared. When he was unprepared, he was barely adequate.

When he entered the auditorium, I could always tell whether or not he'd taken the time to prepare his message. If he had a well-thought-out sermon, he would walk in from the back, come straight down the aisle with his Bible in hand, turn with a smile of confidence, and then begin his message. If he was unprepared (and probably hopeful that God would drop an emergency message upon him), he was insecure. He would enter slowly, pat people on the back, and talk about their sick relatives. He could never remember who they were. One night, he saw this lady who looked familiar. *Sick husband*, he thought. Proud of his recollection, he asked, "And how is your dear husband doing?" "You ought to know," she replied. "You did the funeral last Wednesday."

> As you seek to shape your message, start with something that's already been written: a piece of inspiring literature, a definition of an appropriate word, or a passage of Scripture.

If we wish to be speakers, we need to have something to say that people need to hear, and also be willing to put in the time it takes to prepare the message. Let's assume you have a wealth of personal experience in your head and that your friends say you are a born storyteller. "She's just a stitch!" one woman said to me about her friend. I'm not sure what a stitch is, but this dear woman thought that her friend being a "stitch" was sufficient to make her a good speaker.

Having fascinating stories of your life, a desire to share and a willingness to prepare are solid starting places. But how do they become a message people will want to hear? You need a place to begin as you seek to shape your message. Start with something that's already been written: a piece of inspiring literature, a definition of an appropriate word, or a passage of Scripture.

Using Literature

After Marita's introduction on the first morning of a CLASSeminar, I step up for the opening message. What do I *not* do? I don't waste time on inane comments about the weather, the color of the walls (we recently did CLASS in a room with a mustard-colored stage wall with avocado painted floors), or how I had the flu last week and hope I don't have a relapse "before your very eyes."

When it's time to start, I start. I often begin by reading a quote from Oswald Chambers's book *My Utmost for His Highest*: "Each morning you wake it is to be a 'going out,' building in confidence on God. . . . Let the attitude of the life be a continual 'going out' in dependence upon God, and your life will have an ineffable charm about it which is a satisfaction to Jesus."[1] I call the teaching of this verse my mental warm-up exercise to start the day.

Any time we take a quote of instruction, we need to ask what the reward will be if we follow that plan. So I ask the group, "What will you receive of the Lord if you follow this plan from *My Utmost for His Highest*? What's your reward?" People will be hesitant to respond to this question at first. You have to encourage them to be daring and give an answer. You have to be careful to not frighten them or tell them "that's the worst answer I've ever heard" (or even reveal this by the shocked expression on your face). There are no wrong answers. There are perfect answers, exactly right answers, almost-there answers—and then there are the bad answers, to which you say, "My, what an interesting thought" and move on.

The correct answer to the above question that I pose to the group is "ineffable charm." I congratulate those who got it right, and then I ask, "Who knows what *ineffable* means?" Usually no one does, so I say, "The dictionary says that *ineffable* means 'beyond any type of comparison.' How many of you would like to have charm, better than anyone else's, beyond any type of comparison?" They all smile! They'd all like that. I then share how I once taught charm school. I showed women how to do pivot turns, rise from their chairs gracefully, and frame themselves in doorways. But it was all rehearsed—all nice things to do, but practices not recommended anywhere in Scripture.

I ask the group, "What does the quote from Oswald Chambers suggest we should do to be charming?" Rise up, go out, build up your confidence in God. Chambers states that the first thing we should do each morning to receive *ineffable* charm is to get up. Can't you just see examples from your own life when you didn't get up when you should have?

Chambers also says to "go out." Does this mean that to do God's will you must go out of the house? When I ask the group what "go out" means here, someone always says, "Go outside of yourself." How can we do this? By calling a sick person, writing a note of encouragement, reading a passage of Scripture, or praying for people in need. We need to get outside of ourselves.

By now, the group is into this quote from Oswald Chambers and can hardly wait to share ways that they can build up their confidence in God: studying God's Word, watching for answers to prayer, being open to the needs of others, relying on God's promises.

When we rise up each day with joy and anticipation, get out of our introspective depressing ways, and build up our confidence in God through study and prayer, we'll have that *ineffable* charm and giftedness. The bonus is that this charm will provide a satisfaction to Jesus. Perhaps you're thinking, *Wow! You mean my actions will bring me charm and will make Jesus satisfied with me?* Yes, that's what it means!

Don't you want to start teaching or preaching right now?

Using Definitions

In the study of the Oswald Chambers quote, we looked at the definition of the word "ineffable." Let's base this next section on a definition of the word "class," our seminar title. During my seminars, I explain that during much of our life, we use words in their simplest meaning, paying no attention to their less-familiar definitions. Whatever word you might use to examine, you can often pull a spiritual application from it.

I begin the discussion by stating, "Our name is CLASS. Let's look in the dictionary and see if the definition of 'class' matches what we stand for."

"Class is a group," I say. "Are we a group here today? Good, then we pass the first test."

"Next, 'class' means 'a group sharing something.' What will we share?" People say that I will be sharing as the teacher and that they will be sharing with each other in the small groups, at lunch and during breaks. "Yes," I respond, "but we as a group will be sharing. So, what will we be sharing?"

"As a group," I continue, "we all share the same high quality. How do I know that you are all high-quality men and women?" The audience calls out in unison, "Because we are here!" Someone usually adds, "And we paid a lot of money to come!" I agree and add, tongue in cheek, "Your low-quality friends didn't come. You tried to bring them, but they were afraid to learn something new that might knock them out of their comfort zone." They laugh and nod.

Then I move on: " 'Class' means 'a group *sharing* the same *high quality*, with elegance and style.' Those last two words were not in the dictionary definition of 'class.' I just liked them and thought it wouldn't hurt any of us to aim for a touch of elegance. After all, it is important for us as Christian speakers to keep up somewhat with current fashion. CLASS graduates dispel the world's image of the church lady (hair in a bun, no makeup or jewelry, dowdy long black dress—or the overweight television preacher with too much hair who is busy pounding the pulpit, alienating people instead of winning them over). Simple elegance is a positive goal. We all feel better about ourselves when we know that we look put-together and have a touch of elegance about us."

The last part of the definition of "class" is that it requires *discreet values*. We don't have to carry big black Bibles and bang tambourines on a street corner to have Christian values, because while man looks on the outside, God sees the heart (see 1 Sam. 16:7).

Using Scripture

Each time we open God's Word, we need to ask ourselves three questions: What does it say? What does it mean (in the context of the Scripture)? And, most important in our teaching, how does this apply to me, to you, to our lives?

To teach this, I have to set the stage. Our CLASS verse is 2 Timothy 2:2 in *The Amplified Bible*. My husband used to say that I converse like *The Amplified Bible*. If one word was sufficient, I'd use six. Perhaps that's why I enjoy this version—it sounds like me. In this verse, an older Paul is writing to younger Timothy. Paul has been maligned and tortured for his faith, and he is chained and in prison. Timothy is in Ephesus, and he is not happy that the older pastors he was sent to supervise don't like him. Paul tells him to shape up and get on with the program:

> The [instructions] which you have heard from me along with many other witnesses, transmit and entrust [as a deposit] to reliable and faithful men who will become competent and qualified to teach others also.

I begin by teaching this verse from the standpoint of Paul and Timothy's relationship, looking at the literal advice Paul gives to his young protégé about what Timothy must do before he can come home. Then I show how this Scripture applies to those people who come to the CLASSeminar: They are to take the instructions they hear from me, Marita and the other staff members—along with what they have already learned from their pastors, Bible teachers and others—and transmit this material with a measure of deep faith as a deposit to others. This action is not to be tossed out to just anyone, but to be *entrusted* to personally trained, reliable, tested, proven, faithful men and women who will then become competent and qualified to train and teach others.

As Christian speakers and writers, our message needs to show why studying God's Word can make a difference in people's lives.

Applying this to our attendees, we share how the training that we place into their eager and faithful minds is like a deposit we make in the bank. Our interest is hearing what they do with the teaching as they pass the messages to their friends back home, who will then pass these truths on to others.

Teaching God's Word Effectively

Unless we are teaching the Scriptures from a strictly historical or academic perspective, as Christian speakers and writers, our message needs to show why studying God's Word can make a difference in people's lives. We need to ask, "What is God trying to tell us in this passage?" So often in my years of teaching Bible studies, I've heard people say, "I had no idea that the Bible could be interesting—that it could mean anything to me." What a thrill it is when people begin to get excited over God's Word, apply the lessons to their own lives, and realize that the Bible is not just a stodgy old book for people who are about to die.

As we do at the CLASSeminar, let's take a passage of Scripture and look at it together. We will use 2 Timothy 3:1-7 in the *Good News Bible* (also called *Today's English Version*).

Remember that there will be difficult times in the last days. People will be selfish, greedy, boastful, and conceited; they will be insulting, disobedient to their parents, ungrateful, and irreligious; they will be unkind, merciless, slanderers, violent, and fierce; they will hate the good; they will be treacherous, reckless, and swollen with pride; they will love pleasure rather than God; they will hold to the outward form of our religion, but reject its real power. Keep away from such people. Some of them go into people's houses and gain control over weak women who are burdened by the guilt of their sins and driven by all kinds of desires, women who are always trying to learn but who can never come to know the truth.

First, think about what the passage *says*. Sum it up in one or two sentences. Next, think about what the passage *means*. To understand the lesson, it helps to know who said it to whom and under what circumstances it was said. Here again, as we saw in 2 Timothy 2:2, the old wise teacher Paul is writing to his young discontented protégé.

Timothy was certainly not in an enviable position. He had been sent to straighten out a church disaster that involved people who didn't even like him. Timothy probably said some of the things that we would say in a similar situation: "I thought this would be pleasant working with dedicated Christians. I thought they'd all love each other. The pastors don't even agree, and they wish that I hadn't come. What is wrong with this picture?"

Timothy has cried out to Paul (who is chained up in prison) and basically thinks that life is not fair. Paul agrees that life isn't fair, but tells Timothy, "Let's be real. Let's see life as it is." Paul also reminds Timothy that he wasn't sent to Ephesus for a vacation.

Now, review the passage again with this information in mind. Do you see Paul's perspective? Paul never was one to mince words. He called a spade a spade. He is basically telling Timothy, "Accept life as it is and get on with the program." He has given Timothy's problem some thought and then written a letter to Timothy reviewing the "last days." It is as if he is telling Timothy, "I didn't promise you a rose garden."

We feel sorry for Paul. He shouldn't have to be a cheerleader to a young man at this point in his life. We echo his sentiments to Timothy: "Get on with it." We also feel sorry for Timothy. He was made for better things than this. We understand his desire for Paul to acknowledge his situation and bring him back home.

How does this passage *apply to us*? Is it just an old story of two men who both meant well but had problems? Or does it provide a reality check for us? What is our life like today?

When I teach this passage, I always wish I had more time—because there are multiple messages from my life, from other verses and from today's news that I could share. Each one of us, because of our background experiences, could teach this passage differently. But the point would be the same: We've all got problems.

Let's lay out this lesson in a way that will allow each one of us to see how we can add our own examples or examples from our study participants. As we look at the points within this text, jot down some specific examples of each based on your personal experience and/or current events. (If you were teaching this in a group setting, you would ask participants for examples from their lives.) Then look at the advice that Paul gives to his young protégé.

2 Timothy 3:1-7

Remember, (this is not a surprise) there will be some bad days. People will be:

Selfish _____

Greedy _____

Boastful _____

Conceited _____

Insulting _____

Disobedient _____

Ungrateful _____

Irreligious _____

Unkind _____

Merciless _____

Slanderous _____

Violent _____

Fierce _____

Hateful of Good _____

Treacherous _____

Reckless _____

Swollen with Pride _____

They will love pleasure rather than God. They will be outwardly religious but reject the real power of God.

What are we to do with such people?
> *Stay away.*

Why?
> *They may get into people's houses.*
> *They may gain control.*

Over whom may they gain control?

Weak women [actually, while the passage says weak women, I have seen weak men with these same problems] *who are*:

· *Burdened by guilt of their sins*
· *Driven by different desires*
· *Trying to do right and learn* . . .

but who just can't seem to grasp truth and change their lives. (Do you know any of these people?)

Until we can see the reality of the problems, we are seldom motivated to solve them. This is a lesson of awakening, opening our eyes to the truth. Do you see how you could work off this clear and simple passage of Scripture—or any number of other passages—for weeks? Or at least for one full hour? Can you see how, by using this as a starting place, you could teach a series of lessons on solving life's problems?

What About You?

I hope that as you read this chapter, you asked yourself the following questions: *What do I have to say? Does anyone need to hear this? Where do I start?* You can see that there are many ways to build a message, whether it is by using a classic quote, a definition, or a passage from Scripture.

Ask the Lord to show you if this teaching is for you. Ask for wisdom and excitement. Begin collecting examples from your life, from your classes, from magazines and from world events.

Listen! I hear the call of God on your life.

Note

1. Oswald Chambers, *My Utmost for His Highest* (Uhrichsville, OH: Barbour Publishing, 2006), January 2nd reading.

Discovering Your Communication Personality

MARITA LITTAUER

Since both my mother and I have written volumes about the Personalities, you're probably not surprised to see it here in a chapter title. But maybe you're wondering how Personality relates to communication. What's the connection? Well, our personalities are the filter, or colored glasses, through which we view life. They affect nearly every aspect of our lives—even the way we communicate. So let's spend some time looking specifically at how our Personalities affect our communication style.

In case this is your first introduction to the topic of the Personalities, we'll begin with a brief overview. Even if you are familiar with the Personalities, this may serve as a good review for you. (When I speak on the Personalities, people in the audience often come up afterward and comment on what a good reminder it was for them—or even that they learned something new this time around.)

First, it's important to understand that each of us has a primary Personality and that most of us have a strong secondary Personality. Prepackaged with our Personality is a built-in communication style. Some of us can talk incessantly, whether or not anyone is interested or listening. Some of us are good at keeping conversation to "just the facts."

Others are better at listening than talking and share only on a need-to-know basis. And some prefer to stay uninvolved and are almost fearful to enter into a conversation. Yet in a time of stress, they are the ones to talk to—just the sound of their voice alone is calming.

When it comes to communication, each Personality has areas of great strength—areas in which that specific Personality naturally excels. Additionally, each Personality has areas of weakness that need improvement. As we review these concepts, I hope that you will discover your own communication Personality and its unique areas of strength. We will then examine aspects of your Personality that may need some adjustment in order for you to communicate effectively with others.

The Personalities

There are four basic Personalities. Although none of us fits exactly into one type, we each have a built-in framework—a defined Personality. We come prepackaged; we are each wired a certain way.

The great Greek philosophers first observed the various Personalities more than 2,000 years ago. In particular, Hippocrates noticed that people seemed to fall into one of four Personality groups, each group having its own distinct set of observable traits. The Greek thinkers termed these four groups Sanguines, Cholerics, Melancholies and Phlegmatics. Today, Hippocrates's original teaching has been added to and updated, but the original concepts have proven themselves true throughout the ages.

The Popular Sanguine Personality

People with the Sanguine Personality are the easiest to identify. Another name for this personality type is the "Popular Personality." In this book, we will use a combination of the modern-day adjective and the original term: "Popular Sanguine."

These individuals' loud speech, easy laugh and expressive body language make them easy to spot. Often when I speak on this subject, individuals are able to identify their own Popular Sanguine Personality or that of friends based on just one characteristic—*loud*. In short, Popular

Sanguines are the *talkers* of life and they live for a responsive audience—even if the audience is just the cashier at the grocery store.

The Perfect Melancholy Personality

The next easiest Personality to identify is the Perfect Melancholy—also called the "Perfect Personality." While Popular Sanguines have an open mouth, an open life and open gestures, Perfect Melancholies are just the opposite. Their mouth is closed: They speak only when they feel they have something to contribute. Their life is closed: They share few thoughts or feelings, and then only with those to whom they are especially close. Their body language is closed: They use few gestures when speaking, and those gestures are often short, choppy motions. Perfect Melancholies prefer to think and then speak. They are the *thinkers* of life, and they avoid any frivolous conversations.

The Powerful Choleric Personality

The third Personality type is the Powerful Choleric. These are very busy people—and their communication often consists of commands and orders, with little or no chitchat. They are the Personality for whom the expression "in your face" was created. Their body language consists of pointing, pounding and positioning. They often wag a finger in your face as they talk to you. When speaking to Powerful Cholerics, you may find yourself backing up a step, which will then prompt them to move forward. They also use their fist for emphasis, pounding on a desk or a wall—or they may even pound both hands to make a point. They prefer to stand in a control position, with both hands on their hips as if to say, "Do what I say or get out of the way." Powerful Cholerics are the *workers* of life who expect others to get with the program—*now*!

Do any of these Personalities sound like anyone you know? Perhaps you've identified yourself already. These first three Personalities are the easiest to identify. If none of them seems to fit so far, perhaps the next one will relate to you or someone in your life.

The Peaceful Phlegmatic Personality

Peaceful Phlegmatics are the hardest Personality to identify quickly. They are the people who are steady and balanced, even and consistent. They do not have the extreme traits found in the other personalities. Their voice is softer, and they exude a calming presence. Peaceful Phlegmatics speak only when they have something of value to share, and they are hesitant to offer opinions—yet they can be very convicting or stubborn when they do own a viewpoint. Their body language is relaxed. The Peaceful Phlegmatic uses few or no gestures and will never invade your space (as the Powerful Choleric will). They prefer to lean on something while standing and to recline whenever possible. They are the *watchers* in life, and they often shake their heads in disbelief at the antics of others.

As this book is on communication, not the Personalities, we will present only a quick overview of each Personality type. If you still do not recognize your own Personality type, we suggest that you take the Personality Profile test found in the *Wired That Way Assessment Tool* (available at www.regal books.com and www.classervices.com). If this information is new to you and you'd like to know more, you can read one of our three main books on the Personalities: *Personality Plus*, *Personality Puzzle* and *Wired That Way*.

The Popular Sanguine Personality

Known for their gift of gab, Popular Sanguines can talk anywhere, at anytime, with anyone. This ability to make conversation is a great asset in both personal and professional situations, often making these people the life of the party. However, with these strengths come a few companion weaknesses that Popular Sanguines will need to work on in order to improve their communication with others. The following are some simple steps that the Popular Sanguine can take to be a better communicator.

Limit Conversation

Popular Sanguines need to learn to limit their conversation and allow others the opportunity to talk—even if what they have to say is more interesting and entertaining (at least in their own mind). People who talk constantly can eventually become a bore, even when their stories are entertaining. Popular Sanguines need to work on speaking only when they have something to say that is vital to the situation. Like the little boy who cried wolf, Popular Sanguines who are always talking will not be heard when they have something of great importance to say.

Whenever I am with a Popular Sanguine who has not learned to limit his or her conversation, I am reminded of a principle that I am grateful to have learned from my mother many years ago. She told me that if I were in the midst of a story or conversation and were interrupted, I should just let my story drop. If people were really interested in hearing what I had to say, someone would bring the conversation back to my story and urge me to continue. If no one did, that meant that no one had much interest in the story to begin with. This is a painful lesson for all of us who have the Popular Sanguine Personality—but it helps us to incorporate a necessary discipline into our conversations with others.

> Known for their gift of gab, Popular Sanguines can talk anywhere, at anytime, with anyone.

Tone Down Voice

Another trait of the Popular Sanguine is a loud voice. This is a great asset if you are a public speaker in a room without a microphone. However, in most settings, the loud volume is distracting, irritating and even obnoxious to others. If you are a Popular Sanguine, you need to learn to tone down your voice. "Be beautiful inside, in your hearts, with the lasting charm of a gentle and quiet spirit which is so precious to God" (1 Pet. 3:4).

I am about half Popular Sanguine, and this part of my Personality includes a loud voice. As a speaker, I always considered my voice an asset—that is, until I got married. When my husband (who is a Perfect Melancholy) and I go to a restaurant and I begin to regale him with the events of my day, he notices that others in the restaurant are listening to my story. He shushes me, urging me to speak more quietly.

As I have surveyed audiences, I have found that I am not alone in my loud habits. Those of us who share the Popular Sanguine Personality like having a big audience for our stories—even if that audience has no business listening. I often ask my audiences, "What do we Popular Sanguines do when we discover someone is listening in on our story?" They all shout back to me, "Talk louder!" However, just because everyone else with our Personality speaks loudly, this does not make loudness a trait of effective communication.

My husband has encouraged me to notice other loud Popular Sanguines at parties and other social gatherings. He has helped me to see how unattractive their loud, brassy demeanors truly are. By watching others, I have seen the need for toning down my own voice. And to help me remember to turn the volume down, Chuck and I have developed a code. When I am loud or wound up, he simply and quietly says, "FM." This is a reminder that I need to tone down and talk like an FM deejay. When I am driving home from a trip and am very excited about how a seminar has gone, I practice my FM deejay voice by reading street signs and billboards in a low-key, sultry voice. While I can never really talk like that, practicing to speak calmly and quietly really does help me tone down my voice.

Learn to Listen

Most of us with a Popular Sanguine Personality think that being quiet is the same as listening. In reality, most of us are not listening. We're just working on our next lines.

I once heard that the reason people do not remember names is because they do not care enough to listen in the first place. All the Personality charts tell us that the Popular Sanguines can't remember names. However, I was sure this was not the case for me, so I set out to disprove the theory. I decided that when I met someone new, I would repeat the name within the first few minutes of conversation. I might say something like, "Really, Kathy, how did that happen?" Unfortunately, I found that the theory was correct.

More often than not, when I attempted to use the person's name, I could not remember it! This was not because of bad memory—it was because of poor listening skills!

To train myself to listen better, I humiliated myself several times by saying, "I'm sorry, what did you say your name was again?" It only took a few embarrassing introductions before I learned to listen better. Once I was truly listening, I found that I was excellent at remembering names. So the key for us Popular Sanguines is to *learn to listen*.

The Perfect Melancholy Personality

If you are a Perfect Melancholy, you need to remember that the title "Perfect" does not mean you are perfect, but rather that you like perfection. While there are many aspects of your Personality that are perfect and that others should emulate—such as your deep, thoughtful nature, your need to have the facts straight and the details right, and the courtesy you extend to others in conversation—there are still some areas in which you can improve. As Perfect Melancholies are naturally introverted and tend to keep to themselves, they need to learn to get outside of themselves a little in order to communicate more effectively with others.

Add Humor

Perfect Melancholies are the opposite of Popular Sanguines. While Popular Sanguines need to learn to listen, listening is one of the strengths of Perfect Melancholies. Popular Sanguines are naturally funny, but Perfect Melancholies need to work on adding humor to their communication. Monique, a Popular Sanguine, was recently hosting a dinner party with four guests—all of whom were Perfect Melancholies. It was a gathering of friends who hadn't seen each other for six months, so it was a special occasion. Halfway through the night, Monique couldn't help thinking, *Why isn't anyone else telling funny stories besides me? We haven't seen each other for quite a while and we should be having more fun.* Their conversation was too serious.

She made a mental note to make sure there were more Popular Sanguines at the next gathering. But wouldn't it be great if the Perfect Melancholies could learn to add humor and a light touch to their conversations? They can!

Perfect Melancholies do have a wonderful sense of humor. However, it is a humor that will not be used to entertain, because that seems frivolous to them. We often see it, however, when they teach people a new concept. The Perfect Melancholy's sense of humor will come through as they share true stories about their life and family.

> Perfect Melancholies have a deep and thoughtful nature and a need to get the facts straight and the details right.

If you are a Perfect Melancholy, allow your sense of humor to shine through when you speak honestly about your life. Although you'd probably be hard-pressed to start off each conversation with a joke, you can learn to lighten up. But don't force it, and don't make up stories. Just be yourself. And remember to smile when you are speaking and to laugh at other people's humor as well. As Reinhold Niebuhr said, "Humor is the prelude to faith, and laughter is the beginning of prayer." Even the most serious Personality will benefit from a light touch!

Enter Into the Conversation

Because Perfect Melancholies are by nature listeners and not talkers, they may need to work on participating in the conversation. It is very easy for Perfect Melancholies to feel hurt that no one seems to care enough to ask them what they are thinking or how they are feeling. While it is true that those of us who are not naturally as sensitive as the Perfect Melancholies need to learn to be more caring and attentive, Perfect Melancholies also need to make the effort to enter into the conversation. Perfect Melancholies must be willing to express themselves to others so that their real Personality can be known and appreciated.

Think Positively

The term "perfect" is ascribed to Perfect Melancholies because they desire perfection from themselves and expect it from others. This natural tendency allows them to see all the flaws in people, programs and plans.

My Perfect Melancholy friend Georgia says, "I have to be aware of my tendency toward hypersensitivity. More than once I've misinterpreted a casual remark or oversight of a friend in a negative way. Recently, someone in my social circle sent several friends an e-mail that I did not receive about an upcoming party. When I heard about the party, I assumed I had been purposefully excluded. The truth was my friend had unintentionally forgotten to copy me—but as a Perfect Melancholy, my tendency is to automatically assume the worst."

If you are a Perfect Melancholy, work on offering praise and encouragement to others, rather than criticism. Make an effort to watch for opportunities to build up others. Many Perfect Melancholies feel that endorsing substandard behavior in others will give a signal that it's okay for them to be sloppy in their work, or that a particular behavior is acceptable when actually a change should be made. However, you must realize that people are more likely to change or improve as a result of positive reinforcement, rather than criticism. Memorize Ephesians 4:29: "Don't use foul or abusive language. Let everything you say be good and helpful, so that your words will be an encouragement to those who hear them" (*NLT*).

The Powerful Choleric Personality

Because the ultimate goal for Powerful Cholerics is production and accomplishment, their communication style tends to be brief and to the point. This tendency to be concise is often a strength, as it allows for maximum productivity and minimal distraction. However, Powerful Cholerics often bark out commands with little thought for the feelings of others, who then feel alienated and only too happy to make Powerful Cholerics the first to be "voted off the island." The following are some simple steps that Powerful Cholerics can take to improve their interactions with others.

Be Interested in Others

Powerful Cholerics place a high value on production, so they often see others as getting in the way. In addition, the brusque manner of many Powerful Cholerics can make others afraid to even approach them. All of us who are Powerful Cholerics need to make an effort to improve our communication by treating our colleagues with respect and by being genuinely interested in others.

This can be done in several ways. Start by listening to others. Allow them to complete their sentences and finish their stories. Because Powerful Cholerics are quick thinkers and often know what other people are trying to say, they often have a tendency to cut off other people's sentences and finish their stories—perhaps feeling that they are helping others get to the point. Yes, Powerful Cholerics are always looking for the bottom line! In a fast-paced manufacturing plant, this style of communication might be effective between boss and employee, but that would be the only place. In general, the "get to the point" approach of Powerful Cholerics shuts people down, limits future communication, and prevents them from entering into new relationships.

Marion, a Popular Sanguine, tells the story of how she went to great lengths to find a waitress that her 87-year-old father had made friends with at a resort in Australia. Her father had bone cancer and was in a wheelchair, so Marion had to wheel her father for half a kilometer over grassy lawns, along paths bordered by gorgeous palms, and over a long wooden bridge above a creek. Finally, after a 20-minute trek, they arrived at the café and found the waitress. Later, when Marion began to tell her Powerful Choleric brother all about her ordeals in trying to find this waitress, he looked sternly at her and said, "Did you find the waitress or not?" Like most Powerful Cholerics, her brother just wanted the end result and wasn't interested in any entertaining stories!

So, Powerful Cholerics, take note: This abrupt type of communication has the potential to close the door to any communication, frivolous or functional. Even if you have already heard someone's story before, pay attention! Being interested in what others have to say encourages open communication.

Lighten Up

The old cliché about stopping to smell the roses is good advice for all Powerful Cholerics. Because Powerful Cholerics are so work-focused, they don't take the time to invest in themselves and others. This single-focus approach means that they have limited ability to converse on topics of interest to others. All of their time and energy is taken up by focusing on things that are important to them.

> The ultimate goal for Powerful Cholerics is production and accomplishment, so their communication style tends to be brief and to the point.

A friend once told me how disappointed she had been that, as an adult, she was unable to talk with her father about anything other than his work. Her father's focus on his work had become all consuming, and over the years their communication has dwindled to perfunctory telephone calls and birthday cards. Due to the single focus of his Powerful Choleric Personality, neither father nor daughter truly had any idea what was going on in the other's life.

If you are a Powerful Choleric, you need to lighten up and broaden your area of interest. This might mean watching a bit more TV (especially the news shows—who would think you would have to suggest that someone watch *more* TV?), taking up a sport, or spending more time outdoors—anything that will expose you to something different. As you broaden your horizons, you will find that you share more common interests with others—and therefore are more approachable.

Ask Rather Than Demand

Remember the magic words "please" and "thank you" that you were taught as a child? In the bottom-line communication style of Powerful Cholerics, these niceties are frequently ignored. However, without the word "please" before a request, it often sounds more like a command, and this makes others feel powerless and resentful.

Our CLASSeminar teaching team members Betty Southard and Lauren Briggs were once traveling together to a seminar. One of their flights got cancelled, and they were left scrambling to find a new flight to their destination. Betty, being a Powerful Choleric, soon began barking commands to Lauren. "Do this," she said, "make that call, and see what you can find out from that representative." When Betty taught on the communication style of the Powerful Choleric the next day, she realized that she had been very demanding toward Lauren. She apologized right then and there. She found that it made a good illustration—and was a good reminder to Powerful Cholerics that it is always better to ask than demand.

When communicating with others, those of us who have Powerful Choleric Personalities need to remember the "magic words" and be especially careful of our tone of voice. I am always surprised when words that I thought I said in a lovely and gracious tone are received as if they were a harsh barb. Our true Personality comes through more than we realize. A good verse for the Powerful Cholerics to memorize is Proverbs 16:24: "Kind words are like honey—enjoyable and healthful."

The Peaceful Phlegmatic Personality

Although Peaceful Phlegmatics and Powerful Cholerics are opposites, they do have one thing in common: neither is very expressive. Powerful Cholerics communicate in a brief, sometimes rude, manner. Peaceful Phlegmatics are hesitant to communicate at all, especially with those whom they don't know very well. They are likable, content and lacking in any obvious flaws in most aspects of life—all admirable strengths. Yet, despite their lack of faults, Peaceful Phlegmatics have areas in which they, too, can improve their communication style. If you are a Peaceful Phlegmatic, try the following techniques when you interact with others.

Get Enthused

One of the easiest ways for Peaceful Phlegmatics to improve their communication style is to get excited about something—anything. Of course, such excitement may feel phony to Peaceful Phlegmatics, as by nature they tend to be too low-key. They measure all of life in terms of energy expenditure. Frankly, as my Peaceful Phlegmatic grandmother used to say, they don't think there's much worth getting all "gee-hawed up" about. Yet this is exactly what this Personality needs to do.

If you are a Peaceful Phlegmatic, when someone is kind to you or gives you a gift, be effusive with your thanks. Muster up all the superlatives you can think of. A lack of enthusiasm will cut communication short and cause other people to eventually discontinue their interaction with you because they will feel discouraged by your lack of interest.

> Peaceful Phlegmatics are hesitant to communicate at all, especially with those whom they don't know very well.

Express Opinions

Whereas Powerful Cholerics need to learn to tone down their opinionated nature, Peaceful Phlegmatics need to learn to express their opinions. When Peaceful Phlegmatics are asked what they would like to do, where they would like to go, and whether they would like coffee or tea, their standard answer is typically "I don't care" or "it doesn't matter" or "whichever is easiest."

Many of my friends are Peaceful Phlegmatics, and I have learned that in most cases, they truly do not care. However, because of the tendency of Peaceful Phlegmatics to repeatedly give the "whatever" response, most people give up asking for their opinion and just do what they want. While at first this may seem like a suitable solution, it is a short-term fix that creates long-term problems.

My husband, a marriage counselor, has told me about many of his cases in which a Peaceful Phlegmatic spouse has felt worthless, insignificant and unimportant in the marriage. The other spouse, usually a

Powerful Choleric, long ago took over the decision-making in the home, leaving the Peaceful Phlegmatic to simply take orders and get with the program. While this may have been a relief to the Peaceful Phlegmatic spouse in the early years, a decade or two of being treated as an invisible person often leaves him or her feeling worthless.

If you are a Peaceful Phlegmatic, protect yourself and elicit respect from others. Learn to voice your opinion when you really have one. Maybe you really do not care about coffee or tea, but you probably do care about where you live, where you attend church and where your family goes for vacations. Start by expressing opinions about the things that do matter to you. By doing so, you will gain the respect of others and open lines of communication.

Open Up

While Popular Sanguines spew out more details about their lives than anyone wants to know, Peaceful Phlegmatics tend to be quite closed about the details of their lives. If you are a Peaceful Phlegmatic, you need to open up and share what you are thinking and feeling. Peaceful Phlegmatics are often proud of their stoic tendencies, but those very same cool traits can shut down avenues of communication with others, making you seem indifferent and apathetic. So work on sharing your ideas and projecting your voice.

Who Are You?

As you read through these Personality descriptions, did it become obvious who you are? Could you relate to one particular Personality? If so, you probably also recognized your communication style. And that's a good place to begin.

Remember, communicating effectively isn't just talking, sharing ideas or speaking to others. Communication is a two-way street. We need first to know our natural traits so that we can capitalize on our strengths and work to overcome our weaknesses. As we work to minimize the distracting communication habits that are a part of our Personality, our communication will become more effective.

CHAPTER 3

Communicating with Other Personalities

MARITA LITTAUER

• •

One of the best ways to improve your relationships is to adjust your natural approach to communication when you are speaking with others who have a different communication style. In chapter 2, we reviewed some of the ways that we can easily and quickly identify the Personality of others. As you understand more about other Personalities, you can adjust the ways in which you communicate with them.

Romans 12:18 tells us that the only people we are responsible for are ourselves. The only actions and reactions that we have to be concerned about are our own. We cannot change other people, but we can change the way we approach them. The same holds true when it comes to communicating with others. So let's look at some simple things that we can do when communicating with people who have a Personality that is different from our own.

COMMUNICATING WITH PERSONALITY

WITH POPULAR SANGUINE CHILD

Strengths
They share a zest for life, sense of humor and optimism that can bind them together.

Pitfalls to Avoid
Because organization is not a strength for either child or parent, parent must make an extra effort to instill a sense of discipline and responsibility. Parent must be careful not to compete for the spotlight with the Popular Sanguine children—particularly around their friends during teen years.

WITH POWERFUL CHOLERIC CHILD

Strengths
Parents and children share an optimistic outlook, and a Popular Sanguine Parent is a good "cheerleader" for a Powerful Choleric child who thrives on praise for achievements.

Pitfalls to Avoid
These children will fight to get their way, and a Popular Sanguine parent may give in just to avoid conflict. Being a parent means you will not always be liked by your head-strong, Powerful Choleric, children but if boundaries aren't established and enforced, your roles as parent/child may actually be reversed.

WITH PEACEFUL PHLEGMATIC CHILD

Strengths
You share a relaxed attitude and an appreciation of wit.

Pitfalls to Avoid
Don't expect your Peaceful Phlegmatic children to express excitement over the things you think are fun. Encourage them, but in a loving, quiet way, for they will likely retreat if pushed. You both need to work on organization, so demonstrate self-discipline in your own life.

WITH PERFECT MELANCHOLY CHILD

Strengths
You share a creative spirit and artistic nature. Although you are very different in Personality, you can share a very complementary relationship if you work at understanding one another.

Pitfalls to Avoid
Don't expect these children to be as demonstrative and bubbly as you. Be quiet and take time to listen to them. Offer lots of positive reinforcement for accomplishments. En-courage them in their pursuits, and provide private space and silence for refueling. Respect their need to be prompt, to stick to routines and schedules.

How the Popular Sanguine Communicates with Others

Because Popular Sanguines are natural talkers, tips for improving their communication with others focus on how they can modify or limit their chatter.

Communicating with the Powerful Choleric

When speaking to a Powerful Choleric, the Popular Sanguine needs to stick to the bottom line. When a Powerful Choleric understands that the Popular Sanguine is not just rambling aimlessly—that his or her comments are purposeful and to the point—the Powerful Choleric will perk up and listen.

If you are married to a Powerful Choleric, you may have to work at undoing his or her listening patterns that years of tuning you out have set in place. Don't give up. If you cut out the extra details in your speech and stick to the point, the Powerful Choleric will pay more attention, thereby enhancing your communication. Think of it this way: The Powerful Choleric is the conductor of the orchestra, and you are playing the flute. Never play unless the baton is pointed toward you, and then only play the notes as directed. No sponta-neous solos! Remember what Proverbs 15:2 says: "The tongue of the wise uses knowledge rightly, but the mouth of fools pours forth foolishness" (*NKJV*).

> Popular Sanguines are natural talkers, so they will need to modify or limit their chatter in order to improve their communication.

Communicating with the Perfect Melancholy

When talking to a Perfect Melancholy, the Popular Sanguine needs to be sensitive to the Perfect Melancholy's need for structure and organization. Ruth Crow, a CLASS Graduate and Certified Personality Trainer, found that understanding this basic concept has garnered her a favorable response when talking to Perfect Melancholies. She writes:

> Whenever I had an opportunity to discuss an important topic on the spur of the moment, I would launch into everything I had on my mind. However, after learning the Personalities and recognizing my communication weaknesses, I saw an opportunity to put my newfound knowledge into practice. I needed to contact a school administrator regarding the use of school facilities for a community theater. Even though I had opportunities to stop him in the hall or the parking lot, I resisted my natural inclination to launch into the subject on the spur of the moment. Considering his Perfect Melancholy Personality, I called his office and made an appointment. I organized my thoughts, made some notes and arrived on time for our appointment. He was enthusiastic about the project and agreed to my proposal.

When you are communicating with a Perfect Melancholy, schedule a time to discuss lengthy or important topics. Be careful not to barge in or interrupt a Perfect Melancholy Personality's other activities or conversations.

Communicating with the Peaceful Phlegmatic

When communicating with Peaceful Phlegmatics, Popular Sanguines need to use their natural ability to be positive and encouraging and make a real effort to look for the good in Peaceful Phlegmatics. This means that they will need to think before they speak and curb their natural tendency to just say the first thing that comes to mind.

Cindy, a Peaceful Phlegmatic, still remembers what a thoughtless Popular Sanguine once said to her:

> One day, my supervisor was introducing me to some staff at a nursing home. She said, "This is Cindy, our social worker. She's quiet!" Her words left me thunderstruck. My boss was a Popular Sanguine, and what she said about me was true—I *was* quiet. Yet

I couldn't imagine introducing her to someone and saying, "This is our hospice director. She's very talkative! She never knows when to hush up!"

If Cindy's supervisor had said, "She has a gentle and gracious manner that is wonderful with our residents," she could have communicated her point in a positive way. Instead of alienating Cindy, she would have endeared herself to Cindy.

Peaceful Phlegmatics need to be encouraged for who they are, not just for what they do or what others think they should be achieving. Certainly, offer encouragement and praise about what they do, but be sure that you lift the Peaceful Phlegmatics in your life as well: "Therefore encourage one another and build each other up, just as in fact you are doing" (1 Thess. 5:11, *NIV*). Communicate to the Peaceful Phlegmatics in your life how much you appreciate them and praise them on their ability to soothe the spirit of contentious leaders.

How the Powerful Choleric Communicates with Others

One of the great strengths of Powerful Cholerics is their ability to think and act quickly. However, this very asset is one of the things that often hinders effective communication. Powerful Cholerics need to slow down if they want to improve their communication skills.

Communicating with the Popular Sanguine

When Powerful Cholerics talk to Popular Sanguines, they need to make an effort to be interested in the colorful stories that Popular Sanguines love to tell. Since Powerful Cholerics have an ever-present to-do list in their mind, they tend to view the stories narrated by Popular Sanguines as interruptions. However, when they stop what they are doing and give the Popular Sanguine a few minutes of focused attention, actively listening to the story and responding to their traumas, they will usually find that the stories don't take all that long. As an added bonus, the

Popular Sanguine goes away pleased with the positive response.

Even more important than actively listening, Powerful Cholerics need to be careful not to crush the spirit of Popular Sanguines. Powerful Cholerics must heed Colossians 4:6: "Let your speech always be with grace, seasoned with salt" (*NKJV*). When it is necessary for Powerful Cholerics to instruct or correct Popular Sanguines, they need to do so gently and kindly, curbing their tendency to be blunt.

Communicating with the Perfect Melancholy

Time is also a factor when Powerful Cholerics speak with Perfect Melancholies. Because Perfect Melancholies tend to be detail-oriented and have complex minds, Powerful Cholerics need to give them time to share their thoughts and ideas. The tendency for Powerful Cholerics is to listen long enough to get the gist of the topic and then move on—either physically or emotionally. This habit effectively shuts down communication with all Personalities, but it may send a Perfect Melancholy into a depression.

> Powerful Cholerics need to learn to slow down if they want to improve their communication skills.

Powerful Cholerics should remember Philippians 2:3-4: "Let nothing be done through selfish ambition or conceit, but in lowliness of mind let each esteem others better than himself. Let each of you look out not only for his own interests, but also for the interests of others" (*NKJV*). This is a hard lesson for Powerful Cholerics, but learning and applying it will improve their relationships.

Communicating with the Peaceful Phlegmatic

When Powerful Cholerics communicate with Peaceful Phlegmatics, time is once again a factor. Because Peaceful Phlegmatics do not speak in rapid-fire commands and often take longer to process thoughts than the other Personalities, Powerful Cholerics are likely to dismiss them and shut them out. In this case, the Powerful Choleric needs to work on developing patience and good listening skills.

Betty Southard has discovered what she calls "the seven second rule." When Peaceful Phlegmatics are asked a question, they must take in the information and process it before they can respond. This process takes at least seven seconds. However, Powerful Cholerics have about a three-second tolerance for silence. If the Peaceful Phlegmatic doesn't respond within those three seconds, the Powerful Choleric will often jump in with another question or comment, and the Peaceful Phlegmatic must start the whole process over. The Powerful Choleric will then probably get frustrated and throw out another question or comment. And so it goes.

Powerful Cholerics need to learn to bite their tongue and hold their questions or comments for seven seconds until the Peaceful Phlegmatic can process the request and come up with a response. It just may save the relationship! They also need to show respect for the Peaceful Phlegmatics in their lives by demonstrating to them that their ideas and thoughts are important. They need to resist the urge to speak for them. Respect is all about allowing Peaceful Phlegmatics to be who they naturally are.

How the Perfect Melancholy Communicates with Others

Listening is a natural skill for Perfect Melancholies because they like to process information. However, Perfect Melancholies will need to work on what they say, how they say it, and keep in mind to whom they are speaking. Perfect Melancholies tend to notice the negatives in people and may use a comment about a flaw as a conversation opener—this is not the best way to make strides in communicating effectively!

Communicating with the Popular Sanguine

The Perfect Melancholy's propensity for seeing the negatives in people is especially problematic when they are talking to Popular Sanguines. Because Popular Sanguines crave praise, Perfect Melancholies need to look for opportunities to compliment them. They need to make an effort to praise others and open their conversations with a positive comment, such as "You are always so much fun to be with!" Georgia has learned, "Whenever I interact with my Popular Sanguine friends, I need to remember to *gush*. I have a tendency to *think* wonderful things in my heart and mind without ever expressing them verbally. But just *gushing in my mind* isn't affirming to Popular Sanguines."

Gary Chevalier discovered that his Perfect Melancholy tendency to be analytical had to be holstered around the Popular Sanguines with whom he worked. He writes:

> I work on a church staff with a Popular Sanguine Senior Pastor, a Popular Sanguine Executive Pastor and a Popular Sanguine Youth Minister. My counterparts were constantly postulating absurd, impractical ideas, and I was constantly pointing out the holes in their ideas and explaining how they were impossible to implement. I thought I was sharing my analytical gifts with them and helping them see the flaws in their ideas. Well, before long, my coworkers had dubbed me the "Balloon Assassin." From their perspective, their ideas were like helium-filled balloons that they sent up into the air, just for the fun of watching them fly—and I treated them like clay pigeons and used them for target practice!

While Popular Sanguines are used to having people laugh at their stories, some of those stories sound foolish to the practical nature of the Perfect Melancholy. However, Perfect Melancholies can open lines of communication with Popular Sanguines if they respond to their humor by laughing—or at least by offering a smile or a nod.

Communicating with the Powerful Choleric

Perfect Melancholies enjoy doing research on topics and often have unlimited knowledge on a particular subject. However, Powerful Cholerics are not the ones with whom to share that abundance of information. Perfect

Melancholies need to remember that because Powerful Cholerics have a mental to-do list and try to accomplish more in a day than is humanly possible, they appreciate being given just the essentials they need to make a decision.

When speaking with Powerful Cholerics, Perfect Melancholies should answer their questions with a sound-bite, and then take a breath and allow the Powerful Cholerics time to jump in. If the Powerful Cholerics don't jump in, the Perfect Melancholies can then take over or move on, and then offer supporting details. They can let the Powerful Cholerics know that they have additional information, but it's important that they do not answer questions that the Powerful Cholerics don't ask!

> Perfect Melancholies need to work on what they say, how they say it, and keep in mind to whom they are speaking in order to improve their communication.

Communicating with the Peaceful Phlegmatic

When speaking to Peaceful Phlegmatics, Perfect Melancholies need to focus on the positives and freely offer praise. Words cost nothing! Perfect Melancholies need to remember that they can give positive words away without depleting their "savings account." According to Proverbs, "Pleasant words are like a honeycomb, sweetness to the soul and health to the bones" (16:24, *NKJV*).

When teaching the Personalities at the CLASSeminar, Georgia reminds other Perfect Melancholies that "All too often, we withhold our compliments for only those projects completed with excellence. Instead of waiting for perfection in a task, express your appreciation for the effort, especially to those Peaceful Phlegmatics whose servant hearts are often overlooked."

Too bad Kyle had not heard Georgia's admonition. He tried to fix his Peaceful Phlegmatic wife, Sherry, by giving her a well-rehearsed list of changes that he would like her to make in their marriage to make it perfect. He also gave Sherry a book to read that he believed would help her improve. By the end of the one-sided discussion, he began to see that his Peaceful

Phlegmatic wife had that "deer caught in the headlights" look. He later realized that his wife often had this reaction when too much information was presented to her at one time—she felt bombarded by it. So Kyle then began to present one idea at a time. When she was still reluctant to try his suggestions, Kyle finally sat down and waited for her to give him a response. Eventually Sherry revealed her true feelings and desires about the issues presented. Kyle states, "This tense conversation taught me a lot about presentation style and about giving Sherry focused attention."

How the Peaceful Phlegmatic Communicates with Others

Communication does not come naturally for Peaceful Phlegmatics. They are natural listeners, but true communication requires giving and taking on both sides. Tips for Peaceful Phlegmatics on how to improve their communication with others are all related to what to say and how to say it.

Communicating with the Popular Sanguine

Peaceful Phlegmatics need to remember that Popular Sanguines are inherently creative people. They have ideas popping out all the time. Some of their ideas the Peaceful Phlegmatics will like, while others they will think are complete nonsense. However, it is important that the Peaceful Phelgmatic show enthusiasm when Popular Sanguines have an idea that they think has merit. This may feel phony to them at first, but it will reap rewards for them in the communication department. Besides, it's scriptural—Galatians 4:18 states, "It is good to be zealous in a good thing always" (*NKJV*).

How Peaceful Phlegmatics show their excitement is also important. Their excitement might include a vocal exclamation over the idea's value. They could share the idea with others, giving the Popular Sanguine full credit for creating the idea. They could show physical approval by hugging the Popular Sanguines enthusiastically (Popular Sanguines like touch). Remember, Popular Sanguines don't embarrass easily, and they like being the center of attention.

Communicating with the Powerful Choleric

When Peaceful Phlegmatics talk to Powerful Cholerics, they need to try to speak more quickly than their usual pace. This can typically be accomplished by cutting their standard pace in half. They should never fall into the trap that many of us used when taking a school test composed of essay questions—just writing on and on until we thought that we had enough material to appear to have answered the question. Powerful Cholerics like the basics—just the facts—so they will ask, "What's the answer?" or "What's the point?" Peaceful Phlegmatics should respond to the Powerful Choleric as though they were on a witness stand, remembering the words of James 5:12: "Let your 'Yes' be yes, and your 'No,' no" (*NIV*).

> Peaceful Phlegmatics are natural listeners, so they will need to learn what to say and how to say if they want to improve their communication skills.

As a Peaceful Phlegmatic, Debbie has learned to think through in advance what she wants to tell her Powerful Choleric friends and coworkers. By doing this, she finds that she can give them succinct information and be ready to answer any questions. This prevents Powerful Cholerics from getting impatient with her. She has found this technique to be especially helpful in dealing with her Powerful Choleric boss!

Communicating with the Perfect Melancholy

Conveying information to Perfect Melancholies is different, because they are seldom in a rush. Perfect Melancholies appreciate facts. When speaking to them, Peaceful Phlegmatics should offer them facts and back up those facts with documentation. This is especially important in work situations. Peaceful Phlegmatics should think through information and develop research documentation to have on hand for Perfect Melancholies. This will satisfy their need for facts and will help them feel prepared. They may never need to share the material they have prepared, but the fact that they have it in hand will validate what they are saying.

Making Changes

All of us, regardless of our specific Personality, have areas in which our communication will be easy—areas that are strengths for us. And all of us have areas in which we can improve. After you identify your own Personality and work to improve the specifics mentioned in this chapter for your Personality, you can then work on identifying the Personality of others. This will allow you to adjust what you say and how you approach others for the most effective communication.

CHAPTER 4

Listening, Learning and Leading

Now that you realize you do have something to say that people want to hear, you can choose to continue your personal growth. In addition to studying the Bible and other books, you will gain new insights on how to be an effective communicator as you listen—really listen—to other speakers, teachers, politicians, pastors and even salespeople! You can learn from both good and bad communicators. From the best, you can become inspired to reach higher—and from the worst you can ask yourself, *Do I sound like that?*

Listen and Learn
Florence Littauer

To be an effective speaker, you need to learn how to listen. My favorite method of gathering pithy quotes is by listening to what the average person is saying. I've gotten ideas for new messages from casual comments made by hairdressers, taxi drivers, people in line at the post office, and sobbing women in the ladies' room. If you want new material, just listen.

I learned this technique from my husband, who said to me one day, "Do you realize that when you are talking, you are learning nothing? You already know what you are saying." That didn't hit me well when he said it, but as I thought about it, I realized that I had ignored a wealth of down-to-earth humor that was freely available to me on any trip to the grocery store. And so, I have learned to listen.

Learning new things is also important if you want to be a good communicator. Remember the statement "We get too soon old and too late smart"? I hate to admit that I am getting old; I will forever be working to learn more. There's so much out there that I don't know. I am a perpetual student, and there is little I learn that I can't put to use at sometime. I look at my learning as money in the bank. I put in deposits that don't seem necessary at the moment, knowing that I'll someday make an unexpected withdrawal that will secure the point I am making at the time. I like those surprises, but I know that I can't take out what I've never put in.

You've probably heard the often-quoted figure that most people use only 10 percent of their available brain space in a lifetime. I use this statistic in the CLASSeminar to show the group how much more they could know—if only they would be open to learning. I then ask them to do what I call a verbal visual: "Picture in your mind a common object, such as a 10-drawer filing cabinet." After I ask if they have created one, I say, "If your mind were a 10-drawer filing cabinet, how many drawers would have anything in them?" They all answer, "One." Isn't it a shame that we walk through life with nine empty drawers—space that could be filled with information if we took the time or trouble to listen and learn?

Verbal visuals are helpful because when you give your audience a visual to create, it brightens up *their* brain—*they* have to create. Once they've pictured the filing cabinet, it's theirs. They own part of your presentation. They have customized the cabinet. Once the class has finished visualizing their cabinets, I often ask, "What does your 10-drawer filing cabinet look like?" Some of their descriptions are hilarious. The group is often not only amused but also amazed at how many different filing cabinets the people in the class have constructed. Some cabinets are 10 drawers high; some contain two sets of five drawers; some are five sets of two. In one CLASS, a girl created a filing cabinet in her mind of three sets of three. "That's only nine," one of the men called out. "I know," she replied, "I just threw the tenth drawer away. There was nothing in it anyway."

I've seen people who have created filing cabinets made of oak, mahogany, steel, bamboo and mirrored glass. One girl had little drawers, because she had "small thoughts." You can think up your own verbal visuals. They must be something anyone can picture, and they must be used to communicate a point. They help keep the group awake and give them a sense of ownership of your message.

Leadership in Public Speaking
Marita Littauer

Report after report lists public speaking as one of the top fears of most Americans. In fact, the most recent Gallup poll on the subject lists speaking in public as the number two fear of Americans—second only to fear of snakes.[1] All through school, most people feel terror at the mere thought of having to give an oral report. As adults, their palms sweat and their knees shake when they have to stand up and give a presentation at work or teach a lesson in their Sunday School class.

However, in spite of the grim reports, there are many people who think that being a speaker would be fun and glamorous. They hear the applause, watch the accolades and covet the attention. For the past 25 years through our CLASSeminar, I have been involved in training people to improve their communication skills for both the spoken and written word. While the concepts presented in the program help everyone to improve their basic communication skills, the majority of those in attendance are aspiring speakers. Over the years, we have trained more than 10,000 men and women to be speakers—a big number when you consider that public speaking is something most people fear.

Then there are those people who do not desire to be a speaker but have had the role thrust upon them. Maybe something dramatic happened in their life and, as a result, others invited them to share their story. Maybe God did something in their life that they were so excited about that they could not keep quiet about it. Or perhaps their church was short on people willing to teach Sunday School and they got drafted. At the CLASSeminar, people often share that they feel God is pushing them "kicking and screaming" to some type of public platform. However they get there, willingly or unwillingly, they have ended up on some sort of stage.

The Right Motives

Regardless of the reasons why we may find ourselves speaking in front of an audience, when we look at the arena of public communication, one of the first things we need to look at is our motivation. Why do we want to be in the public eye? When we embark on public communication, we assume a position of leadership and set ourselves up for more extreme scrutiny than others face.

James 3:1 states, "Let not many of you become teachers, knowing that we shall receive a stricter judgment" (*NKJV*). I can attest to the validity of this verse. When we stand up in front of an audience, we become a target for anyone who disagrees with us. I am always amazed at the one person in one thousand who feels compelled to confront me with his or her negative perception of what I have said.

> When we embark on public communication, we assume a position of leadership and set ourselves up for more extreme scrutiny than others face.

I have learned many lessons the hard way as a result of standing in front of a crowd and sharing my heart. I remember one particularly difficult letter that I received after speaking all weekend at a women's retreat. It was two pages long, handwritten in small print. As I opened it and glanced at the first few lines, I could tell that this was not going to be the typical "thank you for sharing with us" letter. As I read, I felt the growing knot in my stomach get tighter and tighter. The gist of the letter was that I had not used enough Scripture in my presentations. Having learned to weigh all criticisms for validity, I went back through my notes.

I had presented four different messages throughout the weekend. In those messages, I had used a total of 38 different Bible verses. I was surprised at how high that number was, because I am more of a biblical principles motivational speaker than a Bible teacher. However, as I shared the various Scripture passages, I recited them from memory or read the verses from my notes. So, because I never read from an actual physical Bible,

I can only assume this woman perceived that I had not used it.

After reviewing the situation, I acknowledged that the comment was not something that I needed to take to heart. But it still hurt. And it did make me rethink what types of events—and audiences—my speaking style is best suited for. But more important, it brought home the fact that our motivation for being a public speaker must be pure, genuine and rooted in our desire to model Christ. If our goals and purposes for being a speaker are not pure, we will never survive—facing these difficulties will wear us down and burn us out.

The ABCs of Public Speaking

Attitude

In examining whether we have the right motives for being a public speaker, I believe that the first thing we need to look at is our attitude. Attitude is the *A* in what I call the *ABCs* of Public Speaking. Our attitude is our inner feelings, our motivation for being up front.

As Christians, our ultimate goal in life should be to be like Christ. The same is true for those of us who are Christian communicators: We want to model ourselves after Christ. As we search God's Word, looking at the life of Christ, we see that He had the attitude of a servant. In Matthew 20:28, Christ says, "Your attitude must be like my own, for I, the Messiah, did not come to be served, but to serve, and to give my life as a ransom for many." That commandment is reiterated in Luke 22:27, where Jesus says, "Out in the world the master sits at the table and is served by his servants. But not here! For I am your servant." At the Last Supper, Jesus served His disciples by washing their feet, a task usually reserved for the hired help. In John 13:14-15, Jesus says, "Since I, the Lord and Teacher, have washed your feet, you ought to wash each other's feet. I have given you an example to follow: do as I have done to you." Clearly, we are to have the attitude of a servant!

As a speaker with the attitude of Christ—the attitude of a servant—we will be willing and even happy to help out wherever and whenever needed.

I started speaking professionally when I was just 19 years old. At that time, my mother gave me some advice that I found very helpful. She said, "Marita, you need to consider yourself in the employment of the person who invited you, or hired you, from the moment you get out of your car or off the plane to the moment you get back in your car or on the plane."

Many times, I have arrived early at the church where I was to speak and found the chairperson in a panic. Perhaps some staff member was sick or had forgotten to do a task. Occasionally, the committee had planned poorly and everything was not as ready as they had hoped. Following Christ's example (and my mother's advice), I joined in and helped with whatever task was at hand. I have stapled packets and set tables. Simply lending a hand can help set the tone for the entire event. It can help calm the nervousness that the committee is experiencing and build an instant rapport with the team.

I once spoke at an event held in the cafeteria of the local junior college. Part of the rental agreement that the church sponsoring the event had with the college was that the ladies on the committee had to do the entire cleanup and leave the room as they found it. When the event was over, the people on the committee set about moving the chairs and tables. While they were busy with that task, I packed up my book table and materials. As I finished, they were beginning to sweep the floors of the massive room. Since the person who was giving me a ride back to the hotel was also on the cleanup committee, I knew that I was going to be there throughout the duration of the cleanup. Without really thinking about it, I picked up a broom and began to sweep. I found myself living out the reality of my mother's advice—considering myself employed by the people who invited me from the moment of my arrival until the moment of my departure.

One of our CLASS Speakers, Raelene Phillips, has put this into practice and, as a result, has encountered very favorable responses. She reports, "I always try to remember how you taught us to be helpful in any area we can when we go to speak. At a retreat in which I was the main speaker last year, I arrived early and helped the staff decorate. One of the women almost had a fit when she found out that I was the speaker. She said, 'Usually our speaker is off by herself in an ivory tower and never interacts with our ladies.' I was so thankful for your training."

Bearing

Next we will look at the *B* in the *ABC*s of public speaking: bearing. Bearing is the outward display of our inner attitude. It is how we come across in our one-on-one interactions with people, not just those in attendance at the event, but also the person taking care of us, the bellmen and the skycaps.

Matthew 5:16 says, "Let your light shine before men, that they may see your good deeds and praise your father in heaven" (*NIV*). For those of us who communicate publicly, this verse is a reminder that people are always watching us. We need to be sure that everything we do is a shining light that leads others to the goodness of the Lord. We are an example, and people watch us!

After attending one of our CLASSeminars, Dawn Whitmore commented, "One of the things that stuck with me was how accessible all of the staff were to the attendees. At the end of the conference, I offered to help pack up, because I saw that the speakers themselves were packing up the merchandise tables. These were real people—not speakers who walked in a half-hour before it was time for them to speak and then were out the door as soon as they finished their portion of speaking for the conference."

Anyone can put on a good act on stage for an hour. But what is needed is for us to have a genuine heart of compassion and a willingness to interact and mingle with the people in attendance. We need to attend all of the sessions of an event, rather than staying secluded in a side room.

My friend, speaker and author Marilyn Heavilin, was a part of the CLASSeminar teaching team for many years. She developed as a speaker during that time, and hearing the teaching on the *ABC*s was part of that process. At all of her speaking engagements, Marilyn meets with the people and gets acquainted with them—even before she speaks.

Marilyn has spoken at many large conferences sponsored by an international ministry. The first few times that she spoke at these conferences, the staff showed her to the speaker room. They told her that they would come for her when it was time for her to speak, and then they left her there alone. Since she was new to this ministry, she followed the rules for the first few conferences. Yet each time she had to sit there alone in this speaker room, she desired to be out with the people, talking with them and finding out what they needed.

After a few conferences with this ministry, Marilyn got bolder. She told the staff that she wanted to be out with the people. The person in charge was surprised, because most of the speakers they had worked with did not want to mix with the people. Marilyn found that as she got out into the crowd and mingled with the people, their reaction as an audience to what she had to say improved. She had built a rapport with them—and they knew her bearing was not an act.

The audience is the reason for our existence as a speaker. We need to remember that they should be lifted up, not us.

Sometimes, speakers will say that they need time alone before they speak to pray or prepare. However, if you are a pro and know what you are doing, that should all be done before you get there. When you arrive at a speaking engagement, you should be prayed up and you should be prepared! Then you can give the people in attendance all of your attention.

One year when I was running the Southern California Women's Retreat, I received a note that thrilled me and broke my heart at the same time. The note said, "This is the first Christian event I have been to where the speakers mingled with the peons—and I liked it!" Her comments thrilled me. I was glad that she had noticed that I always planned this retreat in such a way that the speakers were available. We always held a staff meeting on the Friday afternoon before the retreat started at which I told all my speakers that I expected them to be there for all the sessions, that there was no reserved seating for the speakers, and that they should sit with different attendees at each meal. I wanted them to be at their book tables during all the breaks to sign books and talk with the attendees. So I was pleased that someone had noticed and appreciated it enough to go out of the way to comment on it. (People usually only go out of their way to comment on the negatives!)

But her comments also broke my heart, because she said that this was the first Christian event at which she had experienced such attention from the speakers. This should be standard. Every speaker should mix with the people, just like Christ did. Her use of the word "peons" also concerned me. When we have the attitude of a servant, our bearing should never make anyone feel like a peon. The audience is the reason for our existence as a speaker; without an audience, there is no need for a speaker. We need to remember that they should be lifted up, not us.

Donna Yost, a CLASSeminar attendee, once had the opportunity to go to dinner with the speakers at the end of one seminar. She writes the following about the experience:

After arriving with all the other attendees, we seated ourselves, and there was a space at the end of our table. When the speakers arrived, Florence had nowhere to sit, so she sat down at the space at the end of our table next to me. This was one of the highlights of my life. What a discerning woman! Florence sees people as they are and where they are, and she is not afraid of being in the midst of them. She has "been there," walked the walk, and relates one-on-one with feeling, empathy and encouragement. She knew the people, even without having met them. I felt the same with Georgia Shaffer when talking with her during the seminar. All the staff were so genuine!

Unfortunately, people have been conditioned to think that speakers are somehow far above them. That's why as speakers, it's so important that we do not communicate this message to them. We need to have a bearing that communicates to our audience that we are real, genuine people—and no better than them.

Clothing

The C in the *ABC*s of public speaking is for clothing. You have probably heard the cliché "You never have a second chance to make a good first impression." It is a cliché because it is universally true. However, for those of us who communicate publicly, it is especially true. Think about some of the speakers you have heard in the past. As they walked across the stage to take the microphone, didn't you look at them and make a quick assessment about them before they even opened their mouths? If there was a picture of the speaker on the brochure or flyer announcing the event, it might have even helped you decide whether or not to attend. It is human nature to make an assessment based upon physical appearance.

Each morning that we hold a CLASSeminar, the staff members all line up to introduce themselves to the participants. Whenever I teach this material, I ask the attendees if when they looked at us, they made some kind of assessment about us. Perhaps they looked at us and said to themselves, *Oh, she looks fun; I hope I am in her group* or *He looks like some-body I'd like.* They all raise their hands in agreement that, yes, they had made some kind of decision about us based solely on the way we were dressed and the way we looked. This is why clothing is important.

It is true that, as it says in 1 Peter 3:3, we should not depend on clothing or jewelry for our beauty. However, many Christians have taken this to mean that our outer adornment should be ignored altogether. Yet Scripture also points out how clothing indicates a position of honor or leadership. In Exodus 28:2, God gave specific directions for Aaron's clothing: "Make special clothes for Aaron, to indicate his separation to God—beautiful garments that will lend dignity to his work." Aaron was the high priest, the spiritual leader of the nation of Israel, and he need-ed special clothing that set him apart. As speakers—as leaders—we need to dress in such a way that lends dignity to our work.

In Luke 15, the story of the prodigal son, after taking his inheritance and squandering it on the things of the world, the son decided to return home (see vv. 20-21). In his joy, his father decides to have a celebration feast. He says, "Quick! Bring the finest robe in the house and put it on him. And a jeweled ring for his finger; and shoes!" (v. 22). The fine clothes set him apart and indicate his position of honor.

Likewise, we as speakers need to have special clothes when we stand in front of an audience. At CLASSeminar, we suggest that our speakers dress one notch above the audience, not because they are better than them, but because they are in a position of leadership. We suggest that they find out how the audience will be dressed and then go one step beyond that. For example, if one of our speakers is going to speak at a businesspeople's luncheon, the audience members will probably all be professionally dressed in business suits, so we recommend that the speaker also wear a suit. For women, this should not be a navy blue suit with a white blouse, but something that has a bit more style and makes a statement. On the other hand, if a speaker is speaking at a retreat in the woods for a Christian conference, most people will probably be dressed in jeans and sweatshirts, so we recommend that he or she wear slacks and a sweater.

It's important to dress one notch above the audience, but don't go too far. Many years ago, we once got a negative evaluation on a female speaker who was in a rustic environment but wore silk pants and sweaters with sequins. Her dress set her too far apart from her audience, and the attendees felt that they could not relate to her.

It has been said that if you walk like a leader, talk like a leader and look like a leader, people will follow you. The way you dress honors that position of leadership and will help you to make a good first impression (the appendix features many additional tips on how to dress for the stage for both men and women).

Taking It to Heart

As a speaker, you are always on stage. But as a Christian, your life cannot be an act. You must be genuine—a true follower of the Lord and a neighbor to all. You must be a leader with pure motives; one who understands that the goal of speaking is to change lives. Remember, you have been called to be a servant, not a star.

Note

1. Brian Brim, "The Talent to Communicate," *Gallup Management Journal*. http://gmj.gallup.com/content/content.asp?ci=17683 (accessed March 2006).

Giving an Introduction

FLORENCE LITTAUER

• •

Have you ever wondered how to introduce two people to each other? There they are, standing face to face with each other, with you in between—and you're all feeling somewhat awkward. Each of them is wondering, *Who is this unknown person?*

An invisible wall naturally exists between these two strangers, and you are the one to break it down. You have the opportunity to bring two people together who don't know each other and open up a possible future relationship or a networking opportunity—or at least a momentary conversation. Being the new person in town, in church or in a social group brings out feelings of insecurity, and such an individual is hoping for a rescuer who will break down those walls between him or her and the people happily conversing in the room.

Introducing Others

Whether you are introducing a person to another individual, to a small group or to a larger audience, the principles are the same. The steps follow a simple outline: who, what, where and why.

Who
Beginning your introduction is easy: "It is a pleasure for me to introduce my friend/my brother/my new next-door neighbor/my mother-in-law." After identifying the person, clearly give his or her name. If there is anything unusual about the name, try to give the person to whom you are

introducing that individual something to make it easier for him or her to remember the name: "Littauer is an unusual name, and it helps me to think of it as a tower with lights in it—a 'lit tower.'"

People don't grasp names quickly or remember them well, so repeat the name as often as is natural. Explain your relationship in order to make it clear to others how you are connected to this person. Try something along the lines of, "Some people avoid their mother-in-law, but I have been blessed with an exceptional woman who has become my good friend" or "Mary and I first met when trying on clothes at Macy's. I thought anyone with such good taste should be a friend of mine."

What

Once you have briefly established the person's name and your relationship to him or her, quickly move on to some identification of what this person does or what interests he or she has—something that will open up conversation. For example, you could say, "Bob teaches our Bible study and counsels couples with marriage problems at our church." (Bob will be popular immediately.) "Judy just won the club tennis match." "Rhonda has twin boys in my son's class."

The goal is to mention some quality, job or honor that will give the person hearing the introduction something to converse about with the other person. If you just give the name and walk off, the two are left looking at each other with the unspoken question, *Where do we go from here?* But as you bring additional details about the person's life into the introduction, you create points of contact that the listeners can use to start a conversation.

At a party that Marita hosted, she realized that three men there (all husbands of her friends) were into classic cars. Understanding the importance of a good introduction, she introduced these three men to each other and pointed out their shared interest. Suddenly, this party became much more interesting to them. They now had a common bond that they could chat about. Without a good introduction, they would never have discovered this common link. They would have had a boring time at the party, making polite conversation but nothing more.

Where

Many times, people make connections with the person being introduced when they find out where he or she has lived previously. Say, "Bev and Bill just moved here from New Haven, Connecticut, where he was on the faculty at Yale," and suddenly there's interest. "Oh," someone replies, "my sister lives in New Haven and her son is at Yale right now." Say, "Jane is from Houston, where she was a member of the First Baptist Church," and people familiar with the area will immediately connect with the person. "Did you happen to know Jim Johnson? He taught Sunday School there." It will seldom be the case that Jane actually knows Jim, but by mentioning where the person is from, you open up possibilities for a conversation. Remember, the function of making an introduction is not just to show good manners but also to make a connection between two or more people.

Why

If there is an interesting reason why you brought a particular friend with you to a gathering, it might be helpful to mention that reason when introducing the person.

"Ellie doesn't know a soul in town and I thought the church supper was a great place to start." Or "Paul has a deep interest in the Old Testament, so I knew he'd enjoy this class." Once you understand how simple it is to introduce a friend, there should be no hesitation or awkward moments.

Introducing a Speaker

What if you are called on to introduce the speaker at the spring luncheon, a couple's conference, or the sales training conference? What do you do? Just as I've described above. Whether the introduction is one-on-one or to a larger group, the principles are the same.

Some speakers may have a special introduction already prepared that they will send to you ahead of time. If such is the case, your job will be to read the introduction in such a lively way that it sounds as if you wrote it yourself. However, assuming that you need to create the introduction, you should call the speaker's home or office ahead of time to get the information you need. If this isn't possible, you may have to depend on a quick meeting with the speaker before his or her talk begins. If this is the situation, don't worry—you will be able to put together the introduction on a moment's notice if you remember the principles of who, what, where and why.

Who: "Our speaker today is a delightful lady who entertained me during our lunch together."

What: "She told me stories about her children that made me want to meet them—all nine of them."

Where: "Mrs. Baker comes to us from Boston, where she trained at Lesley College as a kindergarten teacher. I'm sure her training has come in handy with her own family."

Why: "Mrs. Baker is well qualified to speak to us today on raising children, as she has had more practical experience than most of us. Her sense of humor throughout her years as the mother of a blended family and her ability to see the Lord's hand on her life combine to make Mrs. Baker a fascinating speaker. We are grateful that she has taken time from her busy schedule to uplift us today. So help me welcome Becky Baker."

Now that you know how easy it is to introduce a speaker, volunteer to do it every time!

Remember, your job is to break down that invisible wall between the speaker on the platform and the audience below. You provide the bridge between the two. Some of the audience members may have been dragged there and have little interest in the subject; some may be indifferent to life in general. Your introduction is not to be a list of schools the speaker attended (such details are probably in the printed program), but a brief enticement to make even the least-passionate person in the audience excited about what the speaker has to say.

Always end your introduction with something equivalent to "so help me welcome Becky Baker" and then begin to clap for the speaker to signal to the audience that they can start their applause. The clapping will fill in the pause between your introduction and the speaker's opening line and will generate a positive beginning to the speaker's presentation.

When I am scheduled to speak at an event, I always have a prepared introduction sent ahead. However, at least 50 percent of the time, this introduction somehow gets lost and some frenzied person runs up to tell me that he or she has just been told to introduce me. If this person happens to be you, I would have no problem. You would know just what to do!

I could write a book on the different introductions I've been given over the years, including some in which my name was never mentioned. My favorite is the following, which was given by a pastor on a Sunday morning: "Our speaker today is not a real preacher, and what you're going to hear is not a real sermon. In fact, our speaker is wearing a dress, but listen anyway, and don't be deceived by her packaging."

Many years ago, my husband was introduced as the speaker at a men's breakfast. At that time he hadn't written any books, and so his introduction went like this: "Our speaker today is Fred Littauer. His wife, Florence, has written many books, his daughter Lauren has written one book, and his daughter Marita has written several books. It makes me wonder if perhaps we don't have the wrong Littauer here today!" With that he waved at Fred, who then had to rise to the occasion and begin.

As speakers, we always hope that the person who introduces us actually cares and will give us a positive and enthusiastic introduction. It is unfair to any speaker to be introduced poorly. Now that you have read this chapter, you can be that one bright light in the next speaker's life.

Introducing Yourself

Have you ever been in a group situation in which someone decides that you should all introduce yourselves in turn? Have you seen the look of panic that passes over each person's face? Intelligent people suddenly don't know their own names. "There's really nothing much to say about me," some mumble.

But not you! From here on, all you have to do to introduce yourself is state the four Ws that you have ready in your mind. Identify who you are, what you do in life, where you live and why you're there. And don't forget to add your name at the end of your introduction. Why? Think about the last time you met someone new. You probably heard his or her name first. However, since you had other things on your mind, you were probably not listening too carefully. As more was said about the person, you realized that he or she was interesting. Then you began to wonder, *What was her name?* So, when you introduce yourself to a group or an individual, list the interesting details first, and then conclude with, "My name is . . ." People will remember you much better with the information in that order.

Take a few minutes now to think about the four Ws and how to apply them to your life. Store a few facts about yourself in your mind so that when you are called upon to introduce yourself, you'll be ready. You will instantly be the star of the show, because you will be able to speak quickly and with confidence. It takes so little to be above average.

Once you've mastered the art of introductions, you can begin to share with others how they can better introduce themselves and others by using the principles of the four Ws. Then have them practice. At our CLASSeminars, we pair off people around the lunch table on the first day. Each person interviews the person next to him or her and then introduces that person to the table. For some this is simple, but others have never done an introduction before and are delighted to know how easy it really is. This exchange of personal information gets each of them acquainted quickly, and by the end of the third day some say that this sharing time is the highlight of the seminar. In fact, one person said, "I know more about the people in this group than I know about members of my own family."

People everywhere are hungry for personal relationships. Introduce yourself. The world needs to know you!

CHAPTER 6

Selecting Your Topic

Most people get interested in public speaking because something dramatic has happened in their life that is sharable. This is a good place to start. Since you know your own life, you do not have to do much research when you share your story. You also do not need to organize the material or prepare an outline, because you will usually tell your life's story in chronological order.

Other people get involved in public speaking through leading a Bible study group, typically with the help of a study guide that tells them what questions to ask the group and how to conduct the meeting. As with telling your own story, minimal research and organization is needed because the writer or the study has done all the work for you.

While both of these approaches are effective, in recent years, audiences' needs have changed. People's lives have become busy and complex. To be successful in most professions these days, people are often required to put in more than eight hours a day at work. Men are more involved in what goes on at home. And many women now work outside the home. When their careers are combined with their household obligations and personal responsibilities, they no longer have time to go to a meeting just to hear a nice story. Even the life of the woman whose focus is her home has become increasingly full. With fewer women available to assist in the volunteer positions, the stay-at-home mom is feeling stretched and pulled. An event needs to offer more than free child care to get people to commit the time.

Broadening Your Topics

Whether the event for which you may be speaking is a Bible study or a business luncheon, the increasing expectation is that these meetings must offer solid, take-home value. It has been our experience at CLASS that virtually no one calls our ministry and says, "We just want a nice story or a good Bible lesson." Typically, the meeting planner, often a women's ministry leader, Christian education director or pastor, has sensed a real need in the lives of the people. They call us or search the website looking for someone who can meet that specific need—someone who can give a talk that will have real value to those attending.

There is nothing wrong with having a story to tell or being a Bible teacher. However, I hope to encourage you to broaden your range of topics to go beyond just the basics. If you tell your story well or if you are a gifted Bible teacher, you will find that people will assume that you have additional areas of expertise. They will invite you to speak again. You will then need to develop your topics.

This was the case for several different women seeking guidance who came to the CLASSeminar. Each of these women had lost their husbands as a result of the terrorist attacks of 9-11, and now people were asking them to come to various community and civic events to share their stories. These women were not professional speakers, so they were scared to death at the idea of standing in front of an audience to share their emotional stories.

At CLASSeminar, we knew that if these women wanted to continue to speak after the shock of the events of 9-11 had disappeared from people's minds, they would need to have a broader topic base that touched on what God has since done in their lives. As they grow and mature in their faith, there will be new lessons they can pass on to others. So the staff at CLASSeminar worked with each of them to help them craft a message that had meaning beyond the story.

Seeds of Interest

As I mentioned, a good place to start when selecting a topic is to look to your own life experiences. Each of us is unique. We each have different experiences that make us who we are. At CLASSeminar, we call these aspects of our lives our "seeds of interest." Note that I say these are "seeds," as they may not be fully developed. We may not yet be ready to speak on a given topic, but it is something that is of interest to us.

Way back when I had only been married a few years, people would comment, "Oh, you're still newlyweds" when they heard about the nice things that I would do for my husband. The frequency of these comments made me a little indignant. Couldn't I do nice things for my husband after we'd been married a long time? A seed of interest on the general topic of marriage was planted in my mind. Of course, as a newlywed, no one wanted to hear me speak on marriage. After all, what did I know? The seed remained dormant for many years. I was not ready to speak or write on the topic, but the interest remained.

After Chuck and I had been married about 10 years, he went back to school and got his masters degree in marriage and family counseling. He is now a therapist specializing in marriage counseling in his private practice. When we had been married for about 18 years, Chuck and I wrote a book together on marriage called *Tailor-Made Marriage: When Your Life Isn't One Size Fits All*. We have since spoken at marriage conferences and sweetheart banquets. We now sell records of these presentations. I have had a marriage column feature on CBN.com and have written a book called *The Praying Wives Club*, which is all about how to keep your marriage healthy (I also speak on *The Praying Wives Club*). Now a whole branch of my speaking and writing ministry is based on the topic of marriage. The seed that had been planted more than 20 years ago had finally blossomed.

Sean Fowlds, one of our teaching team members at the CLASSeminar, discovered a seed of interest while watching a movie. "I have a presentation I do called *Celebrating the Present*," he states. "The seed for the message was an anecdote from the movie *Tuck Everlasting* that illustrates the idea that life is a gift, which is why it's called the 'present.' In the movie, one of the older characters stresses to one of the younger ones, 'Don't be afraid of dying—be afraid of the unlived life.' The statement profoundly resonated with me and moved me to create what has become my most popular presentation to date. And it all came to me in a theater."

Be alert to what is going on around you. There may be a seed that can grow into a full presentation—spoken or written. Perhaps these seeds are still dormant—or it may be time to water them and watch them grow.

Developing Ideas for Topics

When I am working with a speaker (or potential speaker), I find that reviewing the topics that other speakers are addressing helps them to see how different themes could be developed. This is not meant to steal or copy those other speakers' ideas, but rather to allow what they are doing to inspire ideas in the individual of what he or she could do with his or her interests and expertise.

To help you see how a specific subject could be used, I have listed the following topic categories from the information sheets of many of the speakers that we represent at CLASS. Before proceeding, take a few minutes to study these topics and consider which one might represent a seed of interest in your life. As you review the suggested topics, check off which description particularly hits home. For example, I do not have a degree in home economics, but when I was a child my father was in the restaurant business, so cooking, entertaining and hospitality are important parts of my life. When I review the suggested topics, I check off "hospitality."

Personal Interest
Mental Health

❑ **Depression**

"Oxygen for the Spirit: Breathing Hope into a Tired Life," *Brendan O'Rourke, Ph.D.*

Brendan compares depression to emphysema of the spirit. Recognizing defeating patterns and inviting the Lord to reverse the damage can free people who feel hopeless or burned out. The pure oxygen of God's Word is the basis for transforming the spirit.

❑ **Stress**
"Skipping Over Stones," *Susan Titus Osborn*
Stress can be either positive or negative, but it takes a toll on our bodies regardless. Susan offers techniques for managing the stress in our lives and teaches how to use stress to our advantage instead of allowing it to take advantage of us.

❑ **Emotional Problems**
"Balancing Your Emotions," *Gayle Roper*
What are seven things that might give women difficulty with their emotions? Gayle gives six keys for learning how to control our ups and downs in spite of circumstances.

❑ **Phobias**
"Attacking Fear and Panic," *Dr. Shelley Sysum*
Dr. Sysum educates her audiences on the formation of panic and what needs to be done to beat it. She leans on the premise that God does not desire a spirit of fearfulness for His people.

❑ **Suicide**
"What Can You Do with a Broken Heart?" *Mary Larmoyeux*
Who among us has not walked through at least one of life's major challenges: the death of a child, infertility, the suicide of a loved one, desertion by a spouse, financial problems, a prodigal child, or a major illness? Mary shares stories of God's faithfulness—from both biblical and contemporary times—to help her audiences realize that He is the repairer of broken walls and the mender of broken hearts.

❑ **Compulsions**

"Grace in Addiction Recovery," *Dr. Terry Webb*

Dr. Webb shares how Christians can help and *not* help those who suffer from addictive diseases. She addresses the common questions, *How is God's grace related to recovery from addiction?* and *Can one achieve healing from addictions without going through a 12-step program?*

Physical Fitness

❑ **Weight Control**

"Eating by the Book," *David Meinz.*

New scientific studies are proving the wisdom of the biblical health guidelines that were written thousands of years ago. David Meinz reveals the Bible's secrets on how you can get more energy and maximize your health with today's hectic lifestyles.

❑ **Exercise**

"Fitness for His Witness™," *Laurette Willis*

Laurette covers scriptural keys to health and fitness for spirit, soul and body. She also shares valuable tips she's learned to help people at all levels of fitness get in shape, "Six Seeds to Sow for Vibrant Health," and clever ways to introduce health-giving habits into your family's lives, and outlines the dangers of yoga.

❑ **Diet and Nutrition**

"Fit for His Service," *Jill Jamieson*

In Jill's informative message, audiences discover the four Ds for healthy living— *denial, discipline, devotion* and *dependence*—and why God desires obedience in this vital area.

Spiritual Interests

❏ **Bible Study**

"Don't Wait Till Sunday Morning," *Shawna Marie Bryant*

Shawna teaches the joy of practicing spiritual disciplines such as prayer and Bible study. She kindles a renewed commitment to spending daily time with God and helps people claim the promise of a deeper, more meaningful relationship with God.

❏ **Teaching**

"How to Be the Leader People Will Want to Follow: The Servant Leader," *Kathleen Jackson*

Transform your office or ministry into a group of dedicated team players that will work together to reach new heights! The Servant Leadership philosophy suggests that every person can become a leader by first serving and then, through conscious choice, leading.

❏ **Lay Counseling**

"What to Say When," *Dennis and Ruth Gibson*

The Gibsons provide dozens of techniques that you can use if you find people asking you for personal help and you only have a brief opportunity. Based on Dennis's book *Vitality Therapy*.

❏ **Spiritual Gifts**

"What's My Ministry?" *Sandra Hughes*

When people learn to unwrap their God-given ministry gifts, they begin to flourish in the Body of Christ and understand and relate to other people's gifts and personalities. Sandra encourages her audiences to use their ministry gifts to bless others and live the abundant life.

❑   **Prayer**
"Prayer: Life's Ultimate Privilege," *Shirley Lindsay*
Have you attended seminars offering 10 easy steps to a successful prayer life but found they don't work for you? Shirley's fresh approach to a closer relationship with God focuses on prayer as life's ultimate privilege. You will discover and experience the dynamics of a powerful prayer life.

❑   **Church Administration**
"The Perfect Church: God's Image or Our Imagination?" *Joe Loughlin*
Your church isn't perfect, but don't give up! Using a variety of scriptural images (the Body, the Bride, the flock), Joe refreshes hope and outlook for what God desires to do within and through our churches.

❑   **Emotional Healing**
"This Old House—Remodeling or Restoration," *Dolley Carlson*
Dolley likens our hearts and souls to a house. Are we remodeling by applying temporary fix-ups? Or are we ready for restoration through returning to God the Father's original plan for us?

❑   **Spiritual Warfare**
"Possess Your Promised Land!" *Lynne Drysdale Patterson*
Lynne inspires, entertains, encourages and equips her audiences for the spiritual battles they will face. She teaches how to discover the who, what and where of this spiritual Promised Land that God has given to them along with the how and why they must possess it!

❑ **Evangelism/Discipleship**
"Cross Training," *Jay Schroeder*
Jay relates physical training for optimal athletic performance to spiritual training to experience the abundant Spirit-filled Christian life.

Personal Relationships
Friendship

❑ **Being a Friend**
"The Gift of Friendship," *Janice Brown*
Friends, like gifts, come in all types of packages, and each one is precious and should be cherished. By using the example of Jesus and the relationships He had on Earth, Janice helps people understand the importance of friendship while giving vital steps and interesting hints on how they can nourish the gift of friendship.

❑ **Singleness**
"How to Be Happy and Single . . . When You'd Rather Be Married," *Victorya Michaels Rogers*
It took many years and heartbreaks before Victorya's "prince" finally appeared. Yet Victorya discovered how to be happy in spite of being alone. She shows how people can enjoy the journey of singleness.

❑ **Loneliness**
"Sharing His Secrets: Friendship with God," *Vickey Banks*
God longs for intimacy with each of us, and only an intimate friendship with Him can meet the deepest needs of our hearts. How do you cultivate this kind of friendship? What is God looking for in a friend? Who does He share His secrets with? Vickey answers these questions as she shares the reservation,

the requirements and the rewards of experiencing friendship with God.

❑ **Encouragement**
"Real Angels Give Their Friends Wings," *Linda Shepherd*
"We are like angels with just one wing. We can only fly embracing each other." Linda teaches how to encourage others and how to find and receive encouragement as well.

Marriage

❑ **Meaning of Love**
"Pure Pleasure," *Bill and Pam Farrel*
How to keep L.I.F.E. in Your Love: Love Unconditionally, Invest Strategically with Communication, Forgive Deliberately and Encourage Lavishly.

❑ **Sexuality**
"A Prescription for Romance," *Cheryl Herndon, CNM*
A sexually fulfilling relationship is rare in a society bombarded with emotional exploitation. Cheryl's expertise as a health-care provider and her experience in over 30 years of marriage enables her to provide solid biblically based answers to sexual fulfillment.

❑ **Marriage Preservation**
"Pre-adultery: What a Tangled Web We Weave," *Vicky Olsen*
Why are so many Christian marriages falling prey to adultery? How do two couples who started out as friends find themselves entangled in a web of infidelity? Vicky explores some of the reasons for marital unfaithfulness and imparts biblical and practical tools for safeguarding your marriage.

❑ **The Art of Marriage**
"Planting Hedges Around Our Hearts," *Nancy and Ron Anderson*
The Andersons teach the principles of predicting, preventing and pardoning an affair. Audiences learn the six protective hedges they can plant and grow around their marriage.

Children

❑ **General Advice**
"Preserving Parenting Priorities," *Lauren Littauer Briggs*
The world is attempting to devalue, replace and discredit our role as parents. Lauren's presentation on parenting offers hope and encouragement for making parenting decisions while not losing what makes our children unique individuals or sacrificing our marriages. Lauren offers parents affirmation, tools and qualities for effective parenting.

❑ **Blended Families**
"Tying the Family Knot," *Terri Clark*
Terri relates the hardships and hard knocks of blending families from the perspective of one who went through the fire of divorce, remarriage and step-motherhood herself. Terri shares a message of hope, encouragement and practical application of God's Word to those tying their own family knots.

❑ **Preschool Children**
"Motivating Your Children from Crayons to Career," *Cheri Fuller*
Cheri shares ways to motivate young people without undue pressure and stress. She teaches how to instill a joy for learning and a positive "can do" attitude needed for success in life—including how to encourage late bloomers and under-achievers.

❏ **Discipline**

"Discipline Is the Child's Responsibility!" *Nancy Sebastian Meyer*
Isn't discipline what you want your child to develop in his or her
own life? And while your child matures, you provide external
controls and encouragement. Nancy shows how to help your
child master the art of self-discipline.

❏ **Communication**

"Me and My Big Mouth," *Rhonda Webb*
Rhonda shares how God's Word has something to say about our
speech and how we are accountable to God for every word that pro-
ceeds out of our mouths. She teaches how to be a godly communicator known for wise, encouraging speech, not foolish, idle talk.

❏ **Teen Morality and Pregnancy**

"Your Teen, Your Legacy," *Karie Hughes*
Karie shares candidly the physical, emotional and spiritual con-
sequences of "going too far" along with cutting-edge information regarding sexual purity. She stresses that it's never too early
to gain credibility as you connect with your child by speaking
their love language.

❏ **Older and Adult Children**

"When Your Babies Are Too Big to Rock, L.O.V.E. Them:
Helping Older and Adult Children Through Crises," *Janet Birkey*
As children grow, they go through times of crises, and sometimes we just can't fix it—no matter how hard we try. Janet
guides parents through the steps of L.O.V.E.: Learning to listen to their child's heart; Offering advice carefully; Verifying
the truth of who they are; and bringing Everything to God in
prayer.

❑ **Empty Nest**

"Golden Girls," *Rosa Maria Faulkner*

Do you feel ready for life on Golden Pond? Will you sit out your golden years in the empty nest, thinking that you have completed your service? This message from Titus 2 will inspire senior women to be true Golden Girls using their abilities, insight and wisdom to nurture younger women.

❑ **Grandparenting**

"Grandma Calls Me 'Precious!' " *Betty Southard*

Grandmothers can instill that priceless feeling of unconditional love and acceptance in their grandchildren. However, grandmothers can also end up in the middle of some rather sticky situations. Betty's message equips both mothers and grandmothers to effectively handle any situation with finesse and confidence.

Family

❑ **Dealing with Divorce**

"Celebrating the *Now*," *Candy Abbott*

It may seem impossible to celebrate the now when you're going through divorce, your health is failing, you discover your child isn't "normal," your boss makes unreasonable demands, or you've lost your job and can't pay the bills. Candy shares her secrets to discovering God's joy in the midst of despair.

❑ **Overcoming Divorce**

"Winning Life's Battles," *Carolyn Brooks*

Carolyn shares her real-life testimony of how she traveled through abuse, divorce and financial reversal and came out on the other side a winner and an overcomer. She shares tools to enable women to emerge through any difficulty as radiant, successful women and become all that God created them to be.

□ **Single Parents**

"Single Parents—Hats Off to You!" *Pam Lehtonen*

Single parents have unique and complicated challenges. Pam understands what it means to be a single parent and shares how these unique obstacles can be turned into opportunities to strengthen our relationships with our children.

Suffering

□ **Coping**

"Rebuilding After Shattered Dreams: When Your Heart Has Been Broken," *Georgia Shaffer*

Unwanted change can bring challenges. How do you creatively navigate the obstacles you encounter as you reconstruct your life? Georgia shares a practical five-step approach that can help you or someone you love grow through the pain of setbacks and loss.

□ **Sickness and Pain**

"Survival Skills for the Storms of Life," *Christine Wyrtzen*

Pain is blinding and often debilitating. It renders us inoperable and, worse yet, often gives us the perspective that God is far away and unconcerned about our struggles. Christine has been there and offers seven survival skills from a platform of transparency and an understanding of life's issues.

□ **Death and Dying**

"Good Grief," *Andy Landis and Susan O'Dooley Smith*

Most of us are grieving some kind of loss: death, divorce, job loss, poor health. Andy and Susan lead audiences through the rough road of grief, ministering to both their hearts and their heads with insight on what grief really is, what effect it has on them, and how they can survive it.

❑ **Other Issues of Loss**

"Creating a Culture of Beauty," *Sandy Ralya*

Is your home a retreat from the storms of life? Sandy shares the three ingredients necessary to create a culture of beauty within your home so that no matter how far "over the rainbow" your family travels, they will always say "there's no place like home."

❑ **Recovery**

"Bounce Back," *Diana James*

This heartwarming message provides hope and encouragement to prepare us for, or help us through, times of disappointment, grief, failure or fear. Diana shares spiritual insights and relates poignant true stories of people who give God the glory for enabling them to bounce back.

Personal Goals
Self-Improvement

❑ **Self-image**

"Discover the Real You," *Christy Largent*

How often have you looked in the mirror and just didn't like what you saw? Have you been guilty of not making the most of how God made you? Christy helps people learn about their strengths and weaknesses, their needs and desires, and how to maximize themselves for God's kingdom.

❑ **Conversation**

"The Power of Our Words," *Doreen Hanna*

"Sticks and stones will break my bones but words will never hurt me." We've all attempted to guard our hearts with that well-known statement. Proverbs 19:21 states the truth: "The power of life and death is in the tongue." Doreen presents the influence we have on others through the power of our words.

❑ **Self-control**

"Peace in the Fast Lane," *Renee Bondi*

Have you ever been overwhelmed? Have you ever said to yourself, *I can't handle this! I'm drowning!* Renee gives simple tools to help people keep their day under control and shows how to surrender those difficult times and frustrating days to the Lord.

❑ **Identity**

"Reclaiming the Real You!" *Lee Ezell*

Lee offers a lighthearted approach on how to recover God's original work of art—you! She teaches how to shed those feelings of inadequacy and intimidation so that the real you can stand up.

❑ **Color, Clothes and Fashion**

"Beauty and the Best," *Rebecca Baker*

Rebecca offers numerous tips accumulated from her 15 years of modeling. She teaches how to discover the best ways to fulfill Paul's words in 1 Corinthians 6:20—honoring God with your body.

❑ **Beauty, Makeup and Hair**

"Becoming a Beautiful Woman," *Barbara Anson*

What is true beauty? Can we possess it? Barbara explores natural beauty, physical beauty and spiritual beauty through the seasons in nature, life and our personal pilgrimage, and shows how to incorporate God's standard of beauty into our attitudes and actions.

❑ **Goals**
"Goal Setting: Drawing a Target on the Wall," *Kendra Smiley*
Setting goals is like drawing a target on the wall. You may not always hit the bull's-eye, but at least you will be facing the right wall! Kendra's presentation provides audiences with the basic skills necessary for setting goals in all aspects of their lives.

Leadership

❑ **Qualities of a Leader**
"Women of Purpose," *Pamela Christian*
Pamela examines why, how and where to serve and shows how to have a spirit of pure and devoted service. She shows how to garner confidence in Christ and demonstrates how serving grants fulfillment to believers that can be found in no other way.

❑ **Leadership Models**
"Leadership Secrets from the Presidents," *Jane Hampton Cook*
From George Washington to George W. Bush, presidents have led the nation using different techniques and styles. Jane uncovers these presidential leadership secrets to motivate and encourage leaders and professionals today.

❑ **Leadership Issues**
"How Much Is Enough?" *Bill Weber*
Today's headlines are filled with the tragic stories of people searching to satisfy themselves with material excess. The greed and lust for

things has distorted even the best of us. Bill's biblical look at values helps people get back to basics with God's perspective of things.

Organization

❑ **Household Organization**
"More Hours in My Day," *Emilie Barnes*
Emilie offers the answer to the cry, "There aren't enough hours in my day!" Her teaching provides information on how to make lasting lifestyle changes as opposed to just brief organizational "binges."

❑ **Personal Organization**
"The Time Game: Playing by God's Rules," *Deb Haggerty*
As with the Proverbs 31 woman, today's busy woman will find that a life firmly grounded in the Word of God will enable her to manage her time and priorities in a manner pleasing to the Lord, her family, and her friends.

❑ **Home Decorating**
"Decorating on a Shoestring," *Gwen Ellis*
There has been an explosion of decorating shows on TV, but often the advice offered on these shows is impractical and expensive. Gwen shows how to have a beautiful and comfortable home tailored to your family's style—without breaking the bank—and gives practical pointers for making your home décor your very own.

❑ **Organization in the Workplace**
"Productivity," *Sharon Houk*
What is it about the afternoon "blahs" in the workplace? Sharon puts on her nutritionist hat and discusses proven methods to

beat the after-lunch energy letdown. She also explains how to increase staff output.

❑ **Time Management**
"How to Get Control of Your Time and Your Life," *Sue McMillin*
Sue shows how to get more done in less time—and be better organized than you ever dreamed—using a practical hands-on approach to time management.

❑ **Hospitality**
"God's Word on Manners: Biblical Etiquette for Everyday Living," *Lucy Akard Seay*
Lucy shares practical advice from God's Word on topics such as femininity, home management, manners, hospitality and social relationships. Audiences come away with increased Bible knowledge, tools for applying biblical concepts to their daily lives, and the confidence of God to go forth and implement what they've learned in a variety of practical ways.

Did you find some new topics that you could address? Some areas in which you have an interest, even if it is undeveloped? As you read through the various listings and saw how different people presented specific topics, I hope that you discovered new areas you had not yet considered. Additionally, there are many different ways that a subject can be addressed. As I reviewed the various topics of the speakers represented by CLASS to select the titles presented here, I found many different presentations on the same topic. For instance, self-improvement and friendship are two topics that receive a variety of treatments. Each of us has a unique set of life experiences and a unique perspective—which means that more than one speaker can address a topic.

If you did not check any of the topics in the worksheet, *please do so now before moving on to the next chapter.* As one reader attests, it's an important exercise: "I have found this to be my greatest source of material for my presentations. By honestly rating the appeal of each of the examples listed, I was able to analyze where I've been, where I am, and where I am going. This could possibly save a person a trip to the therapist!"

We can all be grateful that what qualifies us to be Christian speakers is what God has done in our lives and our personal experiences, not the education we have or the degrees we hold.

Researching and Organizing Your Topic

Now that we have seen how many topics there are on which to speak, where do we find the material? Do we have to go back to college? Is this all just too overwhelming? Is this, as my mother used to say, just too much like work? Not if we start with what we already know.

Starting with What You Know
Florence Littauer

Supposedly, we have in our brains everything that has ever happened to us. We have a collection of personal examples to use as our research that could fill notebooks, were we to write them all down. Do you realize that you are storing 30, 50, maybe 70 years worth of colorful stories that can be brought to your consciousness when you make an effort to summon them? Picture God as the operator. You tell Him, "I need a story about my early school days," God presses a few buttons, and there is Miss Prim pointing at you and sending you to the principal's office for something you didn't do. You feel the emotion and see the lesson in that memory.

People learn from our examples. We use colorful stories to bring life to our points. Unless we are stand-up comics, we don't tell a string of stories just to be funny—we do it to teach a lesson. But where do we find our personal examples to prove our points? The following is a list of some sources for you to think about:

- **Hometown Atmosphere.** Growing up in three rooms behind my father's store gave me a humorous and touching base for my childhood stories. Although I didn't like those cramped little rooms, I learned many lessons that I've been passing on for years. For example, my siblings and I had loud voices, a sense of humor and a love for telling stories. Sometimes, our zeal for making fun of people would get us in trouble, as the customer we were talking about would come into the store. When that happened, my father would sing loudly the hymn "Holy, Holy, Holy." We knew that that meant "shut up now!" To this day, if my conversation strays into criticism, I can hear my earthly father singing, "Holy, Holy, Holy" and my heavenly Father saying, "Be still and know that I am God."

- **Nationality Blends.** In this day when families are spread around the country, our children often don't know who they are or where they've come from. My father was born in England, my mother in Canada. My son in law, Randy, has a fervent interest in genealogy and has spent years tracing the backgrounds of our families and teaching his children about their roots. Recently, Randy took my daughter Lauren, their three boys and me to Prince Edward Island in Canada. There, we found records of my grandfather, James Ellis MacDougall, and his 11 brothers and sisters. The postmistress was married to a direct descendant of that family, and she put us in touch with my blood relatives. We visited two homes of these cousins, and my grandsons got a history lesson they will never forget.

- **Childhood Relationships**. My father was my best friend. I loved his English accent and the way he could tell a great story. He taught us tongue twisters and helped us memorize humorous poems that we could recite in unison for the customers. When my brother, Ron, was only three years old, he could recite these poems by himself, and people loved hearing him. I saw a business opportunity and I began charging five cents to hear him talk. One of the favorites was Little Willie:

> Little Whillie had a mirror.
> He lapped the back all off
> thinking in his childish error
> 'twas good for whooping cough.
> At the morning of the funeral
> Mrs. Jones said to Mrs. Brown,
> "twas chilly for Little Willie
> when the mercury went down!"

As I saw how popular his recitations were, I raised his fee to 10 cents. Little did those store audiences know that I would become his high school speech teacher and he would become the top radio personality in Dallas!

- **Education and Training.** I loved reading and studying, got high marks in school, and was awarded a scholarship to the University of Massachusetts. Recently, Marita took me back to visit the campus. I saw the Old Chapel, where I had most of my classes; Memorial Hall, where I worked; and Butterfield Hall, where I lived my freshman year. When I was at the University of Massachusetts in the late 40s, there were 700 students. Now there are 20,000, but the town of Amherst looked much the same. The Village Green bordered the church I attended, the Town Hall and the classic New England inn named for Lord Jeffrey Amherst. As a student with little money, I had always hoped that some day I could come back to Amherst when I could afford a dinner at the Lord Jeffrey Inn. Marita knew my wish and arranged both lunch and dinner at the landmark inn. As we sat at a table for two before the fireplace, I realized what a blessing it is for parents to have an adult child who will give a full day of her life just to be with you.

Now that you are thinking about your hometown, your nationality, your childhood relationships and your education and training, you can see how easy it is to bring these stories to mind and use them as colorful examples. The following is a list of topics that may trigger memories from your own life. Next to each one, jot down some ideas from your own life experiences.

- Talents and hobbies
- Odd jobs and careers
- Courtship and marriage
- Organizations and leadership
- Churches attended
- Christian commitment
- Family circumstances
- Traumas, illnesses and victory

Ask the Lord to retrieve some of these examples that are way in the back of your head, just waiting to be brought up-front and made useful. But don't stop there. All of life that is happening around you is waiting for you to look more deeply.

Organizing Your Information
Marita Littauer

Now that you have a collection of topics that interest you and in which you have some level of personal experience, you have a foundation on which to build. It is time to begin to gather material that will support your seeds of interest. However, before you can get started, you will need to have a plan for how you're going to organize your material.

During the 25 years that I have taught these concepts, I have found that if you just collect "stuff," it merely adds to the chaos in your life. So, before you set to work researching your topics, you need to create a system for organizing and storing the fruit of your research. Knowing that you have a place for storing your information will make you more likely to want to collect it.

Selecting a System

The exact details of the system you develop will be determined by your available space and your Personality. Start by selecting the type of filing system that you think will work best for you. For example, my mother, a Popular Sanguine, does not like to be confined. For many years, she used the "throw it in a box" method, in which she would put all of the information she collected into 8 1/2 x 11-inch copier paper boxes. She found that these boxes were the perfect size for her papers and had a space on the side for labeling the contents.

> Before you set to work researching your topics, you need to create a system for organizing and storing the fruit of your research.

Some people like the accordion files, while others prefer traditional file folders. I suggest using file folders, because they are flexible and allow for growth. If you, like me, find that once you have put something in a file folder you can't find it, I believe that you will find the few extra cents that colored file folders cost to be well worth the investment. Those of us who are at least half Popular Sanguine tend to have a memory for color. While we may not remember exactly which folder we put something in, we will remember what color the file was. When we have a limited number of each color of folder, it narrows down how many files we have to rummage through.

Once you have determined what type of system you are going to use, go back over the topics you checked off in the topics list. Add to that number any other topics you have come up with. Now, go and purchase the items you need to create your system. For example, if you checked off 15 topics, make sure you buy enough files or boxes for each of these—or an accordion file with at least that many slots. Next, label each of the files, boxes or tabs with one of the topics you checked off in the topics list.

Starting Your Research

Now that you have your system in place, you are ready to begin to collect your research. Remember, "research" does not mean that you have to go to the library or spend hours on the Internet. At this stage, I suggest that you do what is called "passive research" by simply being alert to life. Look around you for anything that fits into one of your topics.

One the most obvious places to start your research is by reading books, magazines and newspapers. From now on, you want to be alert, reading everything, anywhere, at any time. You want to look for any articles, facts, quotes or statistics that fit into your personal selection of topics. Even if you think you are only mildly interested in a topic today, be on the lookout for anything that might address it. *USA Today* offers some quick facts on the bottom left-hand corner of the front page, so whenever you have a *USA Today* in your hands, check that out to see if the information provided there is anything that you can use. Skim your local newspaper for articles on the topics of your interest. When you are at a doctor's office, on an airplane or anywhere else that provides magazines for you to read, flip through the offerings—especially if the selection includes magazines to which you do not normally subscribe.

Even advertisements may provide something that fits into your interests. One of my topics of interest is "confidence." I found a long, narrow ad that stated at the top, "Tips, tricks and sound advice for increasing your self-confidence." Since this was one of my seeds of interest, the ad caught my eye. It offered five tips. The first four were truly helpful hints: smiling, wearing red lipstick, standing tall, and dressing creatively. The fifth tip, however, said to protect your self-assurance by using a certain antiperspirant. Still, I cut out that ad.

Now, when I speak on confidence, I open with the world's view of confidence and use that ad as an example. I read off the first four points, illustrating them bodily—I stand tall, I smile, I wear lipstick and, of course, I am dressed creatively. When I get to the antiperspirant line, everyone laughs! Remember, read everything, everywhere, at any time.

Gathering information in this manner will help you track the public's interest in your topics. Magazines spend lots of money on research to determine what the magazine-buying public wants to read. Every item placed on the front cover is there for a reason: Market research indicates that particular topic will make people buy their magazine. Each article inside is there for the same reason: The publishers believe that the topic of that article is of interest to the public.

Keeping this in mind, what do you know if, after collecting articles for a year, you find that one of your files has an inch worth of material and another is empty? You know that one of your topics is hot, while the other is not one that people want to know about at the current time. Armed with that information, get out your inch-thick folder, review the articles and any additional notes you may have added, and put together your presentation. You may even want to write an article of your own. That topic's time has come!

Make Notes or Cut It Out

As you begin to train your mind to look for information that matches your interests, you will be amazed at how much is readily available. As you read, mark any phrases, sentences or paragraphs that fit your topic. Underline them with a colored pen so that they are easy to locate at a later date. Also, in the margin of whatever you are reading, note the corresponding topic and add any comments that the material brings to mind.

This last lesson—making notes as you read—is one that I learned the hard way. One night as I was reading a book in bed, I read a section that I thought would fit in perfectly with one of my presentations. I reached over to the night table to grab a pen, only to find there weren't any there. Since I was all warm and snuggly and did not want to get out of bed, I folded the page in a special way so that I could find it again.

A few days later, I had the book and the pen in my hand at the same time. I went back to that page. I read the front side. I read the back side. I read the page before it and the page after it. Whatever had struck me as so brilliant a few nights earlier was no longer there—or at least I could not find it. I was not in the same frame of mind as I had been when I had originally read the information. If I had underlined and made a notation as I read (as I teach others to do), I would not have lost the words that I thought would enrich my presentation.

As you find interesting items, cut them out. I suggest that you keep both a pocketknife (or scissors) and a colored pen with you at all times.

Perhaps have one set in your briefcase or purse and keep another set wherever you read. Of course, if you are reading a book, you may not want to cut it up, but you can still collect the information by marking the text as you read. Later, make a copy of the page or the pages that feature the desired quote, along with the title page and the copyright page.

If you are reading from a newspaper or magazine, be sure to cut out not only the article you want, but also the name of the publication and the issue date. If you ever want to use that article in a speech, article or book of your own, you will need the source information. For a newspaper, cutting off the top of the front page will give you the needed information. Most magazines include the magazine name and issue information on the bottom corner of every editorial page. If that information is not listed on the pages of the articles you cut out, the cover should give you the information you need. And be sure to keep the complete cover, as one piece—it acts like a folder to hold your article and can be used as a visual during your presentation.

After cutting out or copying the material, you are ready to organize your selections. File your research into the waiting file folders that you have labeled with your seeds of interest. If you want to get really organized, you can take Larisee Lynn Stevens's idea and make it yours: "On the front of each folder, I make four columns: News Articles, My Thoughts and Ideas, Research Info, and Info from Books. When I put something in the folder, I jot down the title and date in the appropriate column on the front. This helps to organize other files on the subject as the file grows. It also gives an idea of the file's contents without having to open the folder."

Write It Down

Another way to gather information is by observing and reflecting on the situations in your life. All of us have things that happen to us, both good and bad, that we think we will never forget. However, as time passes, we may remember that the event happened, but the details begin to get fuzzy.

Keep a pen (or pencil) and paper with you at all times or reserve a section in your PDA to record your thoughts, observations and ideas.

You can also keep a digital recorder with you to capture your thoughts and ideas. If you go the electronic route, you will ultimately need to incorporate these ideas into your paper documents file. As you see or hear something that fits your topic, write it down, input it into your PDA, or record it on your digital recorder. Chris Pingel, a CLASSeminar attendee, writes:

> I keep a small black notebook in my handbag to write down titles of articles from magazines and advertisements. Sometimes, the image in an advertisement helps me think of an outline. One time, I saw an ad that had a picture of an old, worn-out sneaker and got an idea on how to relate that image to our lives. Then I started to notice different kinds of shoes everywhere: high stiletto heels, ballet flats . . . and before I knew it, I had a topic to speak on based on the places we go and the shoes we wear.
>
> Once I trained my mind to look for ideas—to be alert to life—I started a small collection of key rings. The key rings served as excellent speaking props. My favorite Powerful Choleric key ring is "Lead, follow, or get out of the way." Now, every time I am wandering around an airport waiting for a plane, I check out all the novelties for sale.
>
> All of your notes—whether they are about your insights into life or your ideas for speaking props—should also be added to your file folders under the appropriate topic. If you want to file something in two places, you can either make a copy of it or place a note in one file to remind you to cross-reference the other file.

As you go through your day, you may hear other speakers say something that you may like to quote. You may observe an interaction between a parent and a child that illustrates a point that you wish to make. You may have an experience in which you learn a valuable lesson. Any of these incidents can add interest to your speaking and writing—if you can remember them! That is why recording them in some way is so important.

Journaling

Journaling is another wonderful way to gather material on your topics. Some people enjoy writing down the events of their lives on a daily basis. Others find the healthy release of writing down their thoughts, feelings and emotions to be especially helpful when they are going through a difficult time.

It is important to note that journaling is different from keeping a diary. In a diary, you record events, but in a journal, you capture your feelings. Journaling is more than just capturing the facts—it's all about what you do, think, feel and observe. Most of all, it is a reflection and a recording of who you are.

The specific feelings you experience during difficult times are often what give your presentation depth, emotion and validity. Speakers and writers also find journaling helpful because it provides a safe place for them to sort out their "stuff" before they teach others, helps them practice playing with words, and gives their messages a ring of truth. In *Under His Wings*, Patsy Clairmont writes, "Journaling can expedite healing, because our hands are extensions of our hearts, and many times we will write what we wouldn't risk saying."[1]

Journaling can also help you organize your thoughts. Often life's distractions can leave you feeling scattered, but when you take the time to sit and write, you are able to focus and determine what is really important. As a speaker and/or writer, you will find that the ability to capture your thoughts and feeling in a journal is invaluable when you are putting together a presentation that addresses a topic near and dear to your heart. Georgia Shaffer, who often teaches about journaling at the CLASSeminar, writes:

> Many times when I'm pouring out my heart and soul on the pages
> of my journal, I have no intention of ever using that particular

entry in any writing or speaking. However, after 30 years of journaling, I have discovered that those thoughts and emotions communicate and connect with people in ways that my most carefully
crafted sentences can't. The transparency that comes when you are
writing for an audience of one is priceless. Having now used my
journals in my messages, articles and books numerous times over
the years, I can tell you that when you capture the emotional
impact of a moment in a real, honest way, you are most likely to
capture the hearts and minds of your listeners and readers.

To get started, look at your day and write about something that happened that would make a great movie clip. Incorporate all your senses
into your writing so that when you read the entry later, you will be able
to not only see the event but also hear it, smell it, taste it and feel it.
Create a picture with words.

Journaling is something that you don't have to worry about doing
right, because you just write what makes you feel comfortable—what
reflects your shoes-off self. Georgia states, "One day you may write a sentence or paragraph, another day several pages. You don't have to write
every day—journaling is supposed to be fun, not drudgery! You don't
have to write in complete sentences. There will be days you don't feel like
doing it—so give yourself permission to skip that day."

Linda Jewell, another member of our teaching team, also enjoys journaling. She adds, "I just have one rule. Do what works for you." She rec-
ommends first trying different things to see what does work best for
you. For instance, you may want to try out different sizes of journals and
types of papers, such as a small notebook that fits into your pocket or
purse, or an unlined journal if you are also an artist. For easy retrieval of
your journal entries, try dating each entry, leaving a few pages blank at
the beginning of each journal for you to fill in a table of contents (so
that you can quickly locate topics), and labeling the spine or front of
each notebook with either the dates or topics covered.

I find that as a Popular Sanguine, I do not have the discipline or time
to journal every day. However, when I am in the midst of a stressful situa-

tion, writing about what is going on and how I feel is cathartic. For me, this usually takes place when a caring friend, who knows what I am facing, e-mails me to ask me how things are going. Writing an answer to her question allows me to process my feelings as I capture them down on paper. By the time I am finished, I often find that I have written out five pages.

Keep Your Files Updated

Once you begin to speak on a topic, keep updating your files with new material. As you address a specific topic publicly, you may get letters from people on how that message helped them and met their needs. Keep these encouraging notes and place them in the appropriate files. Speaker Bonnie Skinner tells how this system has helped her:

> My life has always been full of exciting and interesting events, and through the years I had accumulated two or three boxes of newspaper and magazine clippings in addition to an abundance of other wonderful memories of my life. However, I had never taken the time to sort through my seeds of interest.
>
> On my way home from attending a CLASSeminar, I purchased 100 manila folders and began sorting through the newspaper and magazine clippings. In short order, my 100 files were labeled. I used a cardboard box as my first filing cabinet and made one rule for filing: pick up the clipping and either file it or toss it. To my surprise, every one of my articles found a home in an appropriate folder. That was the beginning of my filing system! I quickly advanced to a four-drawer filing cabinet, and now I can easily access topics on any subject I need.

Even though Bonnie was often bogged down with scout meetings, carpools, ballet classes, art lessons and other functions associated with motherhood, she is glad that she always remained alert to life. Today, the material that Bonnie collected over the years has helped her to become a retreat leader, a writer and a speaker. "I have the best of both worlds," she writes, "and the Golden Years are definitely the best!"

Fill Your Personal Reservoir

By using this system for researching and organizing your material, you will constantly be filling your personal reservoir. It may be years before you are ready to speak or write on a specific topic, but when you are, you will have already done the research.

People often ask my mother and me how we can write a book so quickly. This chapter is a large part of the answer. We have spent years gathering the information. When we finally sit down to write the book, it is more a matter of putting it all together. We are not starting from scratch—we did the research years ago. The topic is something that we have been filling ourselves with for a long time.

When we sat down to write the book *Raising Christians, Not Just Children* (now *Setting the Stage for Your Child's Faith*), we had at our fingertips more than 20 years of my mother's research on the topic of raising children. She had started years ago with one folder labeled "Children." As she gathered more and more information, the files grew to include one on discipline, one on children and finances, one on adoption, one on family prayer time, and so on.

As we wrote the book, we knew the basic areas that we wanted to address and the order of the topics. The areas became the chapter headings, and the order became the table of contents. We made a new file folder for each chapter. Because we are both visual-thinking Popular Sanguines, we spread the file folders around us on the floor with the chapter titles written inside the open folders. We then took the files representing years of our research and placed them in the right chapter folders.

Each article had already been read, highlighted and annotated, so we did not need to invest time reading through each article. We just skimmed the notes and placed each article or note in the correct folder for the book. Then, one chapter at a time, we put the book together using the notes, quotes and articles we had collected. We spent a little over two weeks writing the book, and it was one of our biggest at the time—more than 300 pages! Of course, since the bulk of the work had been done passively over 20 years, you could say that the book took 20 years to write—not just 2 weeks!

Now that you have a game plan, it's time to get started. Think about what you're interested in and about your life experiences. Choose your topics and begin to research them. And persevere! Bonnie Skinner offers this advice: "If you are at a point where you feel caged in, continue to collect information on items that appeal to you. There will come a time when you will be glad you did!" Start gathering and organizing information on your seeds of interest today, even if you think it will be years before you begin to address that topic!

Note

1. Patsy Clairmont, *Under His Wings* (Carmel, N.Y.: Guidepost Edition, 1994), pp. 122-123.

CHAPTER 8

Putting Power in Your Presentation

MARITA LITTAUER

• •

Now that you have examined your motives, expanded your topics and learned how to organize your research materials, you are ready for the next step. The concepts presented in this chapter will teach you how to take your diverse selection of thoughts and ideas and bring them together to create a powerful presentation—either spoken or written—that will be easy for you to prepare and effectively communicate to the listener or reader.

Having these skills will be an asset to you no matter what you do in life, even if you never plan to give a speech. In the book *Business Protocol: How to Survive and Succeed in Business,* Jan Yager states, "People who can express themselves clearly are at an advantage. . . . This goes beyond using good grammar, proper spelling and appropriate diction in all your communications; you must also speak and write to the point."[1]

There are four parts to putting power into your presentation: passion, personal examples, preparation and presentation. These steps will not only make it easy for you to pull it all together but will also make it easier for your audience to get your message and remember the key ideas you are trying to communicate.

Passion

Many people think that being a speaker is fun or that it is a glamorous lifestyle to lead. They ask, "How can I become a speaker?" I believe you don't really become a speaker; instead, it is an evolution. You don't one day decide that you'd like to be a speaker and then check out books, learn jokes, use other people's material and then reprocess it all into a speech that you call your own. Some people actually do try this approach. Some have excellent acting skills and are able to pull this off, but for most people who try this method, the message is empty. You can tell when you listen to these people that something doesn't ring true.

The best speakers have both technique and passion. But if you can only have one, passion is better. Most of us have heard speakers who were technically perfect; they could win a speech contest because their speech and the delivery were flawless, yet they did not touch our hearts or change our lives. For a while, it was fashionable in the world of professional speakers to work with speech coaches. These coaches had specific areas of expertise—perhaps gestures, pausing, choreography—and worked with speakers to help them perfect their craft. In theory, this sounds like a great concept—don't we all want to master our craft? But I have seen speakers who were better before the coaching. The coaching made them so perfect that all the passion had been coached out of the presentation. On the flip side, I am sure you can recall hearing a speaker who really did not have it all together, but his or her heart was so evident in the message that the message really touched you.

You can learn everything else, but the passion in your message has to come from within. So start by examining your own life. What are you so excited about that you can't keep quiet? What has God done in your life lately that you want to share? The answers to these questions constitute your passion—they are the topics that you are compelled to communicate. They are the natural outpouring of who you are and what you believe. Your passion should be reflected in the seeds of interest you checked off in chapter 6.

When you start with a passion, the other important pieces fall into place more easily. Glenna Salsbury, former president of the National Speakers Association, advises that "your purpose should be larger than your speaking career. Speaking should be a vehicle to fulfill your purpose. Every time you give a presentation, is it springing from your purpose? If so, you are unforgettable on the platform."

Personal Examples

For many years, I have been involved in teaching others how to be more effective speakers. When I observe a speaker who is nervous or struggling, I want to go and hold the speaker's hand. I have seen countless speakers who start out nervously fidgeting with a pen or the change in their pocket, peppering their sentences with "and, uh."

However, I have discovered an almost universal cure for the pain—both mine and the speaker's. As soon as the speaker begins to share a personal story, something he or she knows backward and forward—something that individual doesn't need notes to tell—he or she warms up—and so does the audience.

Speakers become more natural and animated as they tell stories from their own lives. I saw this clearly illustrated many years ago when I was speaking at the first writers conference for which I'd ever been invited to speak. On the front of the brochure were the names of two best-selling authors—a husband and wife team whom everyone had heard of. They were the big names, designed to make people want to pay their money and attend. Everyone was anxious to learn this dynamic couple's secrets.

Their keynote address was scheduled for after dinner and was to be held in the chapel on the college campus where the conference was held. The room's lighting was dim and the pews were hard. If you have done a lot of speaking, you know that this is a difficult setting, even for great speakers. But these noted authors were writers, not speakers. As such, they had written their speech.

They started out standing up front together, behind the lectern, reading their speech. I looked around the room. What do you think the audience's body language was? They were seated in such a way that they were as close to reclining as they could possibly be. They were uninvolved and noncommittal—yet these were the big names the people had come to hear.

At one point, about 10 minutes into the presentation, the wife stepped out from behind the lectern and said, "Let me tell you what happened at our house last week . . ." As she left her prepared presentation and shared a personal example, the energy in the room changed. The audience sat up and physically moved forward. They began to connect with the speaker and get involved. What had changed in the speaker? She became more animated because she was no longer tied to her notes.

> Passion and personal examples are valuable tools, but if you don't prepare, you may gush on enthusiastically with no real point or purpose.

As a speaker, you need the audience to connect with you; they in turn feed you and give you energy. Speaking to a room full of reclining people is draining. But when they respond, laugh when appropriate and get involved emotionally, they keep you going. A good audience makes speaking easy.

CLASS speaker Barbara Anson notes, "I've discovered that if you watch your audience, you can tell when the women shift to making grocery lists and the men begin mentally working on their cars or swinging their golf clubs. Their eyes glaze over. The moment that happens, abandon the facts or the references and give a personal example to keep the audience interested."

Personal examples add energy to your presentation and help you connect to the audience. They let the audience know that you have been there and that you know what you are talking about. Be sure you incorporate them throughout your presentation.

Preparation

Passion and personal examples are valuable tools, but if you don't prepare, you may gush on enthusiastically with no real point or purpose. The key to preparation is to know your topic well and what ideas you wish to communicate, yet be flexible enough to adjust some of your material to fit the specific needs of each group and your assigned time frame. When I first began doing public speaking, my mother told me that I should have 10 hours of information in my head for every one hour I was going to speak. While that rule may sound a bit extreme, it does ensure that you know your topic well!

Many novice speakers are afraid that when they stand up in front of all those people, their minds will go blank. As a result, they write out their speeches word for word. When they stand up front, they actually read the entire message—and it's very obvious that they are reading, not speaking. Most likely, you have heard some of these speakers. I always feel offended that I took my time to attend a program in which the speaker is reading a speech. I feel as if they could have just mailed out the script, and I could have done something else with my time.

Gary, a CLASSeminar attendee, told me a story of how he attended a worship conference at a church that encouraged their speakers to write out their speeches. "I never realized how bad this was," he states. "However, the only parts of one guy's speech that I could stand to listen to were the times when he briefly lifted his eyes from his paper to give a personal example. Another guy read his PowerPoint to us for an hour and a half! Misery! I remember thinking that I could have saved myself a lot of money if I had just stayed home and purchased the speeches on CD! This made me realize that it is much more important to prepare notes instead of just writing out word for word what I want to say."

Notice that I've been talking about preparing a presentation rather than writing one. A good speech should not be written out word for word. It should be prepared with all of the key ideas, teaching, stories and Scripture or other references in the notes, all of which you follow for continuity. By not writing it out word for word, you allow for flexibility in timing, group makeup and the leading of the Holy Spirit to meet the needs of the particular group you are addressing.

The PIER System

The PIER system allows for all of these factors. For those of you unfamiliar with CLASSeminar, "PIER" is an acronym for Point, Instruction,

Example and Reference. Think of yourself standing in front of an audience. You look out at them and a sea of faces looks back at you. The goal is to make your presentation stick out in their minds in the same way that a pier sticks out into the ocean. By remembering "point, instruction, example, reference," you can be assured that all the ingredients needed for an effective presentation are available to you and that you have arranged them to allow for flexibility.

1. Point

As you begin your speech preparation, start with the main ideas you wish to convey to your audience. These ideas become your points which, when collected together, form your outline. As you think about your points, consider how many points you will have in your presentation.

For example, if you have 1 hour for your presentation, 3 to 6 points is a good number to cover in that time frame. Allowing 6 minutes for opening and closing your presentation, 3 points in an hour will give you approximately 18 minutes to develop each point. If you have 6 points, you will have 8 minutes per point with the opening and closing—which is a good pace that keeps things moving right along. If you have 10 points in 1 hour, with an opening and closing, you'll have about 5 minutes per point—which can be done, but it won't give you much time to develop your points. It is possible to fill an hour with 1 point, but you need to be a very gifted speaker to be able to work 1 point for an hour without the audience thinking, *Okay, okay, I've got it now.* My mother is one such gifted speaker who can pull this off, but I wouldn't recommend it for most.

As you begin to prepare your presentation, ask yourself, *What are the key things I want the audience to remember?* Let's say you have three ideas. Take three separate pieces of paper and write one idea across the top of each. At this stage, your ideas may come to you in the form of a question, a single word, a thought or a complete sentence. Don't worry about that yet. Simply write down the ideas as they come into your head.

Since you are writing each point on a separate piece of paper, it doesn't even matter if they are in the order in which you will ultimately use them.

Often, once you get into your preparation, you may decide that the first point you had should be somewhere else. Because they are on separate pieces of paper, you can just rearrange them as you see fit. These ideas become your points, the *P* of PIER. About two inches down from each point, write an *I* in the margin of the paper. Another two inches down, write an *E*, and another two inches down, write an *R*. This creates a simple fill-in-the-blanks type of form to use for your speech preparation.

2. Instruction

Next, think about your point. How are your listeners going to make that concept a part of their lives? What practical guidance can you offer? These ideas will then become your instruction. For example, in your point you may tell your audience that having a good prayer life is important. In the instruction, you will offer them several ways to improve their prayer life. Next to the *I* on your paper, write down the main techniques that you want the audience to learn. Since these ideas are something you have studied or experienced, they will be concepts you know well. Therefore, you don't have to write out long, cumbersome instructions. By listing just the key steps, you can glance at your notes and be reminded of the things you intend to communicate.

Because the instruction often involves things that are familiar to the speaker, it is typically the element that most speakers do not do well. The speaker knows what he or she is talking about, so the tendency is for him or her to also assume that the audience is just as familiar with the material. Therefore, he or she does not develop the instruction completely. The reality is that if the audience knew what the speaker was going to talk about, they wouldn't have come to hear him or her speak.

So don't overlook this portion of your preparation, but spend some time working on the instruction. Be sure that your notes are clear and that you can expand on a given instruction if needed. Depending on the time allowed for the presentation, you may ultimately give detailed instruction and even have the audience try your suggestions right there. Or you may simply give the audience the techniques needed to implement your ideas—making the session into more of a workshop environ-ment. Offering listeners an idea without equipping them to accomplish it will be frustrating to the audience and futile for you.

3. Example

If you give the listeners the point and instruction but quit there, you may come across as preachy and hard to relate to. To show the audience that you know what you're talking about—that you've been there—include a personal story that exemplifies the principle. You may share your own struggle with the situation to show how you overcame it, or the example you give may be from the life of a friend or family member. People remember stories better than they do just points.

When preparing this part of your presentation, remember that these stories will usually be about your own experiences, so you won't need to write them out word for word. Next to the *E* on your notes, jot down a few key words to remind you which stories you intend to tell with that particular point. If you have a lot of time, you may want to include sev-eral stories to make your point. Or, if your time is cut at the last minute (which often happens), you can pare down your stories and just tell one—or even use an abbreviated version, if necessary.

You can also adjust your stories so that they are appropriate for the particular audience you are addressing at the time. For example, if the group is made up of men and women, be sure to use stories that will relate to both. If it is all women, you may use slightly different examples. They will feel as though you customized the presentation just for them. The stories will give your points life!

4. Reference

So far, all we have discussed are your own ideas. The reference portion of the PIER system allows you to back up what you are saying and give it more authority. For example, if your presentation is being given to a Christian audience, you should include various Scripture passages as your references. You may have one verse you will want to quote or even several that will validate your point.

As you prepare your presentation, next to the *R* on your notes, list the location of the verse or verses you wish to use. If you are only using a couple of verses, you may want to write them out completely in your notes so that you can quote them without having to fumble through your Bible while you are up front. If your time is cut, you can simply offer the audience the chapter and verse of the passage you are using and paraphrase it to save time. If you have been asked to stretch your message (which also does occasionally happen), you can ask someone from the audience to find the verse and read it to the group.

For this portion of your preparation, I strongly recommend that you use Bible software. Most of us have spent a lifetime in church and are familiar with many Bible verses, but frequently we do not know where that verse is located. Bible software allows you to type in a key phrase of the verse or even just a word, and it will bring up all the verses in the Bible that have the elements you are seeking. Once you select the correct passage, you can simply copy it and paste it into your notes, and the verse reference automatically comes with it. Additionally, the software allows you to compare different versions and choose the one that is most appropriate for expressing your point.

I have found the software to be a boon to my preparation. When I was working on my Bible study *Journey to Jesus*, I wanted to use the verse that talked about how "not many of you should become teachers, as you will be judged more harshly than the rest." I pretty much knew the verse. For years at our CLASSeminar, I'd attributed the admonition to Paul, and no one ever challenged me on it. However, when I wanted to include that passage in the book, I needed the actual reference. So I went to my Bible Explorer program, keyed in a few words and told it to search the Pauline Epistles. Nothing came up! I spoke firmly to my computer, telling it that I knew the verse was located somewhere in Paul's letters. Then I expanded the search to the entire New Testament. Lo and behold—there it was in James! No wonder it did not show up in a search of the Pauline Epistles. For years, I'd been attributing it to Paul in error.

If you have Bible software that you use and love, great! Get it out and use it often. But if you do not currently own any—and you are computer literate—I suggest a simple and inexpensive program called Bible Explorer. It will do everything most of us as Christian speakers and writers will ever need. (You can get more information on Bible Explorer at the CLASS website: www.classervices.com.)

In addition to the Bible, there are many other references that you can use to reinforce what you are saying, including newspaper or magazine articles and books. When you quote from a magazine article, have the actual article in your hand and read from it. The visual stimulation adds variety for the audience and affirms your source.

If you have collected the articles together with their covers as suggested in the previous chapter, show the cover briefly as you read the article. If your eyesight is such that reading the fine print while you are standing in front of a group is difficult, write the quote on a large sticky note and place it inside the magazine cover so that it will appear that you are reading the actual article.

> If there is no continuity between the points in your presentation, they are not as clear for the audience to catch or as easy for them to remember.

Additionally, statistics or quotes from notable people work well and will add variety to your presentation. I recommend that every speaker have a good quote book, such as *Bartlett's Familiar Quotations*, in his or her resource library and have several quote websites bookmarked. A good one to start with is www.allaboutquotes.com. This is a portal to a vast array of quote websites that allow you to search by topic or keyword. George Barna is also a good source to obtain research on topics that are likely to be of interest to speakers (see www.barna.org).

When you use these additional references, be sure to list the sources in your notes. You don't have to include the source of a quote or statistic in the verbal presentation, but you should have it in case anyone questions the validity of the information.

Building an Effective Presentation

After you have filled in all your blanks, the next step is to make your points easier to remember. As the speaker, you could give your presentation with one point being a question, another being a single word and another being a thought. However, when there is no continuity between your points, they are not as clear for your audience to catch or as easy for them to remember. So go back over your points. If three of your four points are questions and one is a single word, rework the idea that the single word represents into a question so that the points are uniform. Or, if there is no obvious pattern to your points, try to boil the points down to one or two words that represent the main thought.

Then review your points again. Do several of them start with the same letter? Do a couple of them rhyme? Can you use the first letters to spell a word that summarizes your overall message? If you see a pattern emerging, try to make the wording of the other points fit that pattern. This is where a thesaurus or a synonym finder is helpful. If you have one or two words that don't fit the pattern, look them up. See if you can find a synonym that will communicate the same point that will fit within your pattern.

I often use three points to teach this concept, which I obtained from an article on father-daughter relationships by Gary Smalley. These are: (1) A father should include meaningful touching as his daughter grows up; (2) A father who wants to develop a close relationship with his daughter should invest himself in her best interest; and (3) A father should keep his anger under control.[2]

Now, quickly cover up that paragraph and try to repeat those points without looking. You can't, can you? While those are three excellent points, they are too long and cumbersome to be easily remembered.

So let's look at the first point. Can you condense it into one key word? How about the word "touch"? Now, let's look at the second point. There are several key words you could pick out, but since the word we have chosen for the first point begins with a T, can you think of a T word that captures the heart of that point? How about "time"?

Okay, we've arrived at the last point. What *T* word comes to mind for this one? Most people come up with "temper." It does capture the essence of the point, but does it fit with the other words? Each of the simplified points should be the same part of speech or in some other way consistent with each other. For example, they should be all nouns, verbs, adjectives, thoughts, statements or questions. To check this, simply use the point in a sentence. "A daughter needs touch." "A daughter needs time." Those first two points both work. However, the third point, "A daughter needs temper," doesn't fit the pattern—"touch" and "time" are nouns, but "temper" is a verb. How can you rework it so that it fits the context, is a *T* word, and is the correct part of speech? Try, "A daughter needs tenderness." Now you have three easy-to-remember points: touch, time and tenderness. The message is the same, but now it is also easy to remember!

Benefits of Using the PIER System

In addition to helping you organize your presentation, the PIER system also allows you to connect with audience members of each Personality. By using this formula, you know that you have something in your presentation for everyone!

- **Powerful Cholerics** want the *points*. They will appreciate the fact that you have succinctly outlined your main ideas and that you have provided lots of documentation.

- **Peaceful Phlegmatics** need *instruction*. They will respond to the instruction in your presentation, especially if you clearly show them how to do something and demonstrate how easy it is to do it.

- **Popular Sanguines** respond well to *examples*. They like to get to know people personally and will respond well to the personal illustrations you use in your presentation—especially if those illustrations are humorous.

- **Perfect Melancholies** want the *references*. The facts and details that you use will ensure that they are satisfied with your presentation.

Betsy Jabola, a speaker and ventriloquist, uses the PIER method for a variety of presentations and has had great success. She writes:

Whenever I do a program for Sabbath school, children's stories, chapels, even banquets and bridal showers, I always use the PIER format. I start out with the main point in mind and develop stories (using the puppets with ventriloquism); then I find songs, object lessons and games to serve as examples and instruction; and then I use lots of good references to back up the program.

Whenever I have helped other people come up with programs for Sabbath school, I always use the PIER acronym and show them how they can come up with their own program with confidence. I've taught in Sabbath school for 18 years and have helped a lot of people get started learning how to put together programs when they feel panicked. PIER is an invaluable tool!

Patty Lauterjung used the PIER formula this way:

One month after attending the CLASSeminar, I had to prepare a speech for Toastmasters on the topic of "Speaking to Entertain." The goal was to entertain the audience through the use of humor drawn from personal experience and other material.

My Perfect Melancholy Personality found it hard to think of myself as entertaining. It was difficult for me to even start the speech. I knew, however, that most professional speakers use humor. I was determined to learn how to entertain people, knowing it would help my husband's and my financial seminar business. Talking about budgets, goals and debt can be very boring!

As I sat brainstorming with my husband about my speech, the PIER outline suddenly came to mind. We came up with the point: the frustrations of grocery shopping. I decided to begin my speech with, "What is it that really irritates you about grocery shopping?" I then made a list of every example I could think of, from waiting in line to clipping coupons.

The references and examples added body to the speech. Building stories around tissue and toothpaste drew the audience in by helping them relate to my experiences. A quote about toilet paper from Andy Rooney of *60 Minutes* brought the house down and served as the climax to my speech. I ended the presentation with three points of instruction summarizing how to effectively handle choices.

Not only did PIER help me prepare a speech, I also actually won both a local and a divisional Toastmasters Humorous Speech contest—and had fun in the process! For Perfect Melancholies like me, I recommend using PIER to break the writer's block. The other Personalities will also benefit from the organization that PIER will bring to their ideas.

After learning PIER, Larisee Lynn Stevens told me, "You summed up in one chapter what it took me three or four years to learn in Toastmasters. After I majored in speech and drama in college and spent eight years in Toastmasters, you taught me a better way to write a speech." I hope that you also gain from this process and do not have to learn the hard way!

Presentation

Once you have filled out your form using the PIER formula, your speech is basically finished. When you are ready to actually present your message, you will need an opening, which may be a story—the *E* in PIER—or a question that helps to create a need in your audience for the topic you are presenting.

The Opening
If you begin with a question, be sure that it is a question with an obvious answer and one that everyone present can answer affirmatively and without embarrassment (this same principle will be true for all questions you

might ask throughout the presentation). I remember sharing the platform with a speaker who asked the audience lots of questions. But because she had not set them up properly by making the answers clear, the exercise fell painfully flat.

When I begin my presentations, I always ask the audience, "How many of you have noticed that there are people out there who are different from you?" To indicate that I am expecting a response to the question—in particular, a raised hand—I raise my hand as I lean into the audience and ask the question. Of course, everyone has noticed this fact, so they can all answer by raising their hands in agreement. By asking a question to which they can all respond, I have already done two important things: First, I have created an atmosphere of interaction. Rather than having a sense of being preached at, the audience is already involved and interested. Second, since the question is something that applies to everyone, the communal response draws the audience together.

The Presentation

After your opening story or question, move right into your points. Remember, PIER is a formula, not usually an outline in itself. However, as Patty Lauterjung has shared, if the speech only has one point, PIER could become your outline. By preparing your speech using PIER, when you actually make your presentation, you can start with the example—the story—and then move into the point that you learned from the story. You can then teach the audience how to apply that point in their own lives (the instruction) and wrap it up with a quote or Scripture.

Further, you can arrange the point, instruction, example and reference any way you want, and you can present it differently each time. In the example from Patty Lauterjung, she started with the point, added the examples, gave her reference (the quote from Andy Rooney), and closed with the instruction. This flexibility allows you to make each presentation unique and fresh and target it to a specific audience.

If you choose to use a handout for your presentation—which I suggest because it allows your audience to follow along and provides them with a place to take notes—use the points of your outline to make up your handout. If you are using Scripture passages or quotes, you may also want to include these in a smaller font next to the key points. This keeps you from losing people in the audience as they lean over to the person next to them and ask, "What verse was that?" In addition, by including the chapter and verses on the handout, you can skip them when you're pressed for time without the audience losing that valuable part of your presentation.

If you do choose to use a handout, be sure to include your name, address and phone number to identify whose material the audience is taking home. This way, if they want to quote you at a later date or use your ideas in some research of their own, they know how to find you to get permission. Plus, if they love what you said and want to recommend you to another group, they will know how to contact you.

The Closing

Finally, you will need a closing. Your closing might begin with a recap or a summary of your points and end with a challenge or call to commitment. Often, a poem or other inspirational piece that exemplifies your message is an effective closing. (If the closing quote or poem is not something that you wrote, be sure to cite the source.)

Many people who give a Christian message in a church or church-related setting feel that they should close with prayer. However, unless the presentation is an actual sermon, I suggest that you not use a prayer as your final words. The reason is because in our society, the way we show appreciation to a person who is on the stage—a performer, singer or speaker—is by giving them applause. However, closing with a prayer creates a somber and quiet mood. Most of us are not accustomed to breaking into applause at the sound of "Amen," so when you close with prayer, the audience doesn't know whether they should thank you with applause or keep quiet. It creates an awkward and uncomfortable moment for everyone.

If a prayer of confession or commitment is appropriate after your presentation, there are two effective ways to handle it. One is to have the emcee or program chairman say the prayer after you have finished. Or, toward the end of your presentation, you can offer the prayer that is on your heart but then come back with your summary of points, closing poem or concluding challenge. This provides an effective transition from the prayer mood to a powerful closing and will leave your audience on an up note.

Of course, occasionally the desired mood may be a quiet, somber exit into a time of reflection or stillness—what I call the "kumbaya" moment. In such circumstances, the prayer may be the most effective way to close.

Expect Anything and Everything!

If everything goes as expected, you should now have a perfect presentation. However, perfection is seldom a part of a speaker's world. There are too many variables. The speaker before you takes too long . . . the food service is late . . . the entire program has started late. While the speaker is usually the one the people have come to hear and the one the meeting planner has built the entire program around, he or she is usually last on the schedule. All of the delays in the other parts of the program now become the speaker's problem. So, when this happens, do you take all of your time and have the meeting end late, or do you finish on time?

> If everything goes as expected, you should now have a perfect presentation. However, perfection is seldom part of a speaker's world.

When this occurs to speaker Marilyn Heavilin, she always asks the meeting planner, "Do you want what you paid for, or do you want me to be done on time?" Phrasing the question this way helps to put it in perspective. Sometimes, the meeting planners say, "Take all the time you need." Other times, they tell Marilyn that they do need to be out of the room by a certain time, so she has to trim her presentation.

If the meeting planners tell you that you need to trim your speech, you may be in trouble if it has been written out word for word. I am sure that you have heard speakers whose time had been cut give as much of their presentation as the time allowed and then say, "Well, we are out of time. If you want to hear the rest of the message, you'll have to buy the book" or "You'll have to buy the tape." I always feel cheated when I hear this because I have invested my time and my money to hear a professional speaker. I want to hear the presentation in its entirety.

If you have prepared your speech using the PIER formula, you can be flexible. If you are using handouts that list the Scripture passages, you can easily cut them from the spoken presentation. You can delete the magazine articles that you were going to refer to and trim the number of stories you were going to tell (or even skip them on some points). In this way, you can easily cut your speech in half without the audience ever knowing!

As I mentioned previously, the PIER system also more easily allows room for the Holy Spirit's direction. After all, He knows the needs of the group better than anyone else! When you have prepared your speech rather than written it out, you can have variations without stress. Sometimes I find myself saying words that I had not intended to say or sharing a story that was not in my notes. As the words are coming out of my mouth, part of my brain is saying, *Where did that come from? That is not what I usually say here.* Almost always, someone comes up to me afterward and says, "You know what you said about——? You said that for me. It was just what I needed to hear today." Thank You, Holy Spirit!

Practice

Once you have found where your passion lies, peppered it with the vitality of personal examples, prepared your message and put the presentation together, you need to practice delivering your presentation. Start alone in your bedroom or office, preferably in front of a full-length mirror. Allow that passion to show itself and use hand gestures to clarify your points. I suggest that the gestures you use be specifically tied to the words you are speaking at that time. Any time you use a number in your speech, hold up that number of fingers. If you say something like, "He spoke so softly, I could hardly hear him," hold your hand up to your ear.

I have found that if you pretend that the audience is deaf and is reading your lips, you will use your hands to attempt to aid them in their understanding. By doing this, you create effective gestures that will replace distracting or repetitive chopping motions.

If speaking is new or uncomfortable for you, work on your message until you are comfortable with all the parts. Then record it. Listen to how you sound. You are likely to find places where you have lots of gap fillers such as "uh" and "you know." These usually indicate an area in which you are not as familiar with your material or are not as comfortable with it. Make changes or study those areas more thoroughly.

It is unlikely that you will ever be completely happy with your finished product, so the next thing that you need to do is to give your speech in front of supportive, but honest, friends or family members. This may be three people in your living room, or it may be your Bible study group at your church. Ask for their encouragement and insight (notice that I didn't say *criticism*!). Accept their praise and listen to their suggestions. If they have suggested a number of changes, you may want to practice delivering your speech once more in a controlled environment before you venture beyond the safety of your support network. If they give you a thumbs-up, move forward. Share what God has put on your heart with others and expect results!

CLASS graduate Andrea Chevalier found that even though she is a teacher and speaks frequently, practicing her presentations helped her feel at ease in a situation that was out of her comfort zone. She writes:

> Recently, my pastor asked me to help him preach the "female" side of his sermon topic. To help me feel more at ease, I decided to practice my portion of the sermon in the pulpit at the church when other people were around the building to give me a small audience. I even practiced with the microphone on so that the sound of my voice coming over the speakers would not scare me on the big day. I went through my part of the sermon until I felt I had worked out all of my nervous feelings. When Sunday came, my part went great. I know that the fact that I had already

taken the time to get comfortable with my surroundings had a lot to do with it.

Even if you are a pastor or someone who is comfortable in front of an audience, practice can be an important tool to help you determine the pacing of a specific story. Before you speak, stand and deliver any parts of the presentation in which you might not feel totally confident. This may be in your home or office or in a hotel, but do the gestures and add your vocal variety—just like you would in front of a live audience. If time is a factor, time that module to see how long you need to allow for that section.

Chris Pingel was ready to give a speech. As advised, she practiced it the day before. She told me, "After hearing the presentation, my husband said that it was too 'teachy' and needed to be more 'touchy.' So I went back to the PIER process. Fortunately, it only took me two hours to redo my notes because PIER made it so easy." When you prepare your speech using the PIER system, you can be confident that you have included everything that you need for a strong presentation and still have freedom and flexibility—which is the sign of a real pro!

Notes

1. Jan Yager, *Business Protocol: How to Survive and Succeed in Business* (Hoboken, N.J.: John Wiley and Sons, 1991), quoted in "Book Summary," *Spirit Magazine*, January 1992, p. 22.
2. Gary Smalley, "Fathers and Daughters," *Fullness*, March/April 1986, p. 24.

CHAPTER 9

Putting Heart in Your Presentation

FLORENCE LITTAUER

• •

A few years ago, I was a judge for a speaking contest. One young man had done an excellent job. He looked good, was well-dressed, spoke clearly, used appropriate gestures, and smiled mechanically on occasional humorous lines. He had obviously spent a lot of time on his preparation, and he only glanced at his notes a few times. Yet there was something missing. His message had no heart. When he finished his speech with a challenge to the audience, people weren't moved to follow it. As the judges met, he was mentioned as one of the best, yet when we voted, no one put him in first place. Why? He just didn't make us care. We weren't moved to action or touched in our hearts.

Have you heard a speaker like that—one who was technically perfect but didn't move you in one way or another? Would you give him the Blue Ribbon?

When we started CLASS in 1981, we didn't have a lesson on putting heart into the message. I assumed that everyone who wanted to be a speaker (especially a Christian speaker) had a passion for his or her subject. Yet I found that our attendees would often ask me, "How is it that you are able to show your heart? How do you touch my heart so deeply? How do you put such feeling into your words?"

I didn't have an answer, because I didn't have a teachable technique. It was just something I had always been able to do. I hadn't taken lessons or meditated over the possibilities—I just did it. How could I teach someone a skill that just came naturally to me?

How to Reach People

When you can't come up with an obvious answer to this question, it's time to pray for a solution. So I prayed, "Lord, You've given me this ability and You've called me to train others, to teach them all I know. I've held back nothing, but I don't know how to give my passion to those who don't seem to have it. Please show me how to share this passion with others. In Jesus' name, amen." Within a few days, I began to see some ways I could teach others how to reach the hearts of their audiences.

1. Establish Need

The first step is to establish a need. Unless people see their emotional needs, they won't be motivated to change. For example, when a person gets along with everyone and is the most popular person on the block, he or she doesn't look for new skills or ways to change. Or when people convince themselves that all their problems are someone else's fault, they want those other people to get help. But when their mate threatens to leave, their children reject their attention, the boss says they have no people skills, or their best friend tells them that they've had it with them, they may then be open to looking at themselves and asking, *What is it about me that causes people to turn away?*

The bottom line is that whatever topic you are teaching, try to establish with your audience that they need to hear it. When I speak on marriage or give my testimony, I often start by saying, "Before I married Fred, I read several romantic novels. They all ended with the line, 'and they got married and—'" I put my hands out toward the audience, and they call back, "lived happily ever after!" To which I reply, "You say that in a very depressed tone. I can tell you've tried it." My comment and their response establishes the need. I don't have to say, "Listen up. You need this."

When I speak on overcoming depression (based on my book *Silver Linings*), I ask, "How many of you know at least one person who is depressed?" About every hand goes up. They need to know what to do for this person—who may be themselves.

Another way that I establish need is by talking about the problems in the world today: "Remember, the Bible says that in the last days there will be . . ." By doing this, I am able to establish that there are great needs in the world today and that the Lord is calling us to meet those needs. I spend a relatively short time on the problems and then move on to our purpose and then on to our plans—what are we preparing to do about the problems.

If everyone were problem-free, there would be no need for Christian speakers. The problems give us a purpose.

2. Give Personal Testimony

It is the personal story that validates the material being presented, so it is important to give enough of your personal experience in order to be believable. When I speak on the Personalities, I give examples of how Fred and I didn't understand each other when we first got married. I wanted to have fun while Fred wanted everything to be perfect, and I felt that perfect was no fun. Learning about the Personalities opened our eyes. I realized that just because Fred was different didn't make him wrong, and just because I was fun-loving didn't make me frivolous. We learned to appreciate each other the way that God had made us.

When I speak on depression, I know what I'm talking about. I gave birth to two sons who were both fatally brain damaged. How did I live through that tragedy? How did it affect our marriage? Audiences want us to share our heart's burdens and backgrounds with them through stories. When we do this, we're not trying to be emotional; we just want our audiences to know that we have not lived fairy-tale lives. We've been there. We've worked through problems. We are real people.

Not all speakers have believable stories. I once sat next to another speaker who had her notebook open on the table. I couldn't help but notice a red arrow in the margin, under which was written the words, "Cry here." To reach the hearts of people, we must be sincere. People are astute enough to spot phonies.

Although your teaching isn't all about you, there needs to be enough testimony to show where you've been and what the Lord—or the material you are presenting—has done in your life.

3. Present a Plan

It's not enough to establish need and share your heart. You can't leave the audience focused on problems—yours and the world's. You need to answer the question, So what are we going to do about it? Your answer must outline a plan that includes some possible steps toward reaching a solution. You can never guarantee the plan you present will always work for everyone, but you can say, "Here are some steps that have changed my life [or my marriage, my attitude, my parenting, my depression]."

> As speakers, we must offer a ray of hope. Regardless of the topic we are presenting, we must give people a way out.

If you are having trouble coming up with a plan, review the pages of this book. This book is filled with steps you can take to improve your mind, your vision, your view of God, your relationships, your speaking skills, your sincerity, and your ability to touch the hearts of people.

4. Offer Hope

Old-fashioned preaching had us all afraid of going to hell if we didn't march down the aisle—today! Many people came to the Lord through this approach, but in today's churches, people are often most afraid of what's going to happen tomorrow in this life on Earth. Will their spouse be faithful? Will their teenagers stay out of trouble? Will they be able to pay the mortgage? Will they ever get beyond their credit card debt? Can they ever get over this feeling of depression? Will they ever laugh again?

As speakers, we must offer a ray of hope. Regardless of the topic we are presenting, we must give people a way out. These are good people who are overwhelmed, unappreciated, overextended. What do you have to offer them? Is there a light at the end of the tunnel?

We can't just say, "Pray about your problem and it will go away." We all know about the power of prayer and know that God can perform miracles, but we can't promise what the Lord will do in a given situation. I've met several women who have left the Church because a well-meaning person told them that their husband's philandering was because they hadn't prayed enough, or gone to the altar enough, or given enough.

Christians are discouraged and need a glimmer of hope from you. I hope that this book will give you enough fresh hope that you can pass it on to others through your teaching, your prayers and, most important, your love.

5. Call for Commitment

As you near the end of your message, give a challenge for change. In some situations, such as when you are in a church, the pastor may want you to do an altar call, or he may want to do it himself. Most of the time I'm left without instructions, so I give a verbal challenge based on my topic or on Scripture. I encourage people to follow the steps I've offered and, if appropriate, continue to pray for the healing of their problems. I pray with them and ask the Lord to bless each one there and touch them in their specific area of need. At CLASS, we have a commitment letter in the back of our workbooks for each person to fill out. They are not promising their future to us, but as a commitment to the Lord.

6. Expect Results

Let your audience know throughout your message that you are counting on them. Tell them that you know they want to do what's right and that they will work for change. As you review your main point at the end of your talk, reaffirm your faith in them that they will not let this time be wasted and that they will go out with a renewed spirit, new hope and new commitment to accomplish the task at hand—whatever it may be.

We have faith that you will listen to the Lord's call and follow His good will. He will then shine through you and give heart to your message and vibrancy to your presentation.

Trouble in River City

After creating these six steps on how people can reach the hearts of others, I realized that salespeople actually use these steps to make a sale—even though they may not realize it. One of my favorite musical comedies is *Music Man*. I saw it twice on Broadway and I have the video. The whole plot revolves around an engaging salesman, a con artist, who sells band instruments to people who didn't know they wanted them. Here is what he did:

1. *Establish Need*—When he comes into River City on the train, he jumps off with his salesman's case in hand and heads for the village square where the women are gossiping. He wants to sell trombones to these women, but because he knows that not one of them will want to buy one, he really has to be creative in order to establish a need. So, he tells the mothers that there are "troubles in River City"—that their boys are smoking and basically headed down the road to ruin unless they step in and do something.

2. *Give Personal Testimony*—What can they do? "Don't worry," he says. "I have the answer. I'm going to start a boy's band so that your boys have something to do after school and stay out of trouble. I've been setting these bands up all over the Midwest with great success."

3. *Present a Plan*—He then offers to take care of the problem in no time. "Here's what we'll do," he says. "You give me the money and we'll get the instruments to you in no time. And the trombones will lead the big parade."

4. *Offer Hope*—He next reiterates how prevalent the teen problems are, but he promises that together, they can make a difference: "We will keep the boys out of the pool hall and have them practicing their music."

5. *Call for Commitment*—Next comes the call for action. "For just a small price, I will bring you the 76 trombones and the uniforms. Just give me the money and I'll be on my way." The mothers are so eager to cure the problem that they didn't even know they had that they happily give him the cash.

6. *Expect Results*—Finally, he tells the parents that if they buy these instruments and form a boy's band, they will be so proud of their sons. "You will be so excited when you see little junior march on to the field in his red uniform with gold braid. This will be the biggest day River City has ever had."

If you've seen the musical, you probably know the rest. The salesman repents and turns from his ways so that he can marry Marian, the librarian.

I thought that I had come up with a new idea when I first wrote down these six steps on how to reach people's hearts and promote change. But what I thought was new has actually been around forever. Maybe it didn't have the same labels, but the concepts are universal. It is emotional truth. Some use these truths for good and some use them for devious purposes.

I was a little disappointed that I hadn't been the first person to discover these concepts, but I then wondered, *Is it in the Bible?* As I prayed for an answer, the Lord gave me assurance that He'd been reaching hearts long before I ever thought of it. I laid out a pad of lined paper and a pen by my bed so that I'd have it handy when the Lord spoke to me. To make it easier for the Lord, I wrote down the six points, spread out over two pages. I prayed that whatever part of Scripture had these points would be revealed to me in the morning. I thanked the Lord ahead of time for His answer and went to sleep.

When I woke up, I was like a child who hoped Santa Claus had come in the night. As I opened my eyes, the book of 2 Timothy was on my mind. I flipped to it in my Bible and saw clearly what Paul had written to Timothy:

1. *Establish Need:* You need help over there in Ephesus.
2. *Give Personal Testimony:* I've been hurt myself. I know what it's like.
3. *Present a Plan:* Here's what I want you to do.
4. *Offer Hope:* This plan will give you hope.
5. *Call for Commitment:* I ask you to promise that you'll follow this plan.
6. *Expect Results:* I won't be around long, so you need to take over the ministry. I know you can do it.

So my steps weren't new—and neither are our troubles. During our CLASSeminars, we ask participants to fill out a chart that lists a number of "troubles" that they or a family member have experienced. We total these up and give the top five or six troubles of the group. They are shocked when they see that about 50 percent of their family members have been divorced, and that there are high rates of alcoholism, drug use and depression. As I share the totals, I emphasize that these statistics are from us, Christians, not from New York City or from Hollywood. These are problems from our own River Cities. But wouldn't it be great if we could help people in the areas of their real troubles, in their own River City?

> My steps aren't new—and neither are our troubles. As speakers, wouldn't it be great if we could help people in the areas of their real troubles?

Come to Me Soon

There are two possible approaches to teaching a lesson based on the Bible. First, you can start with the Scripture and pull a lesson out of it—the Bible to subject method. I did this in chapter 1 when I took Paul's admonition to Timothy, "Remember that there will be difficult times in the last days" (2 Tim. 3:1) and developed a lesson for Christian leaders out of Paul's words. Second, you can choose your subject and then look for scriptural support—the subject to Bible method. I did this in the section above when I outlined the six steps and then prayed for the right Scripture to give authority to the points. As I read 2 Timothy, I saw how perfectly it fit my outline.

Let me give you an example of a lesson that I use at the CLASSeminar. As you look at the outline, assume that *you* are going to teach it as Paul's advice to Timothy and offer *your* advice to the audience. Notice that I have listed the four Ws (who, what, where and why) from chapter 5 to help you introduce the material to your audience and that I listed the Bible verses that fit each point.

How to Reach the Hearts of Your Listeners

Who: Paul to Timothy
What: Personal letter
Where: Rome to Ephesus
Why: To encourage and instruct

1. Establish Need

1:7	You need to be encouraged.
1:8	Don't be timid.
1:8	Don't be ashamed.
3:1-5	These are bad times.
3:13	Evil men will grow worse and worse.
4:3	They won't listen to true teaching.
4:3	They will do their own thing.
4:4	They will make up new religions.

2. Give Personal Testimony

1:8	God appointed me as an apostle-teacher.
1:11	I suffer constantly.
1:12	I'm not ashamed, for I know and trust the Lord.
1:15; 4:10-16	Everyone has deserted me
2:9	I am chained like a criminal.

4:6　My life is about over.

4:7　I've done my best.

4:7　I've kept the faith.

4:8　I'm waiting for my crown of righteousness.

4:17　The Lord stayed with me and gave me strength.

4:17　He rescued me from the lion's mouth.

4:18　He is taking me to heaven.

3. Present a Plan

1:13　Hold to the true words.

1:13　Keep the faith.

1:14　Use all the good I've taught you.

2:2　Train teachers who will train others.

2:4　Be a loyal soldier for Christ.

2:14　Don't fight or argue.

2:15　Study God's Word for His approval.

2:16,23　Don't enter into foolish discussions.

2:21　Be a clean vessel for special use.

2:22　Avoid the passions of youth.

2:24-25　Be a kind, patient and gentle teacher.

4:5　Keep control of yourself.

4:5　Endure suffering and keep going.

4. Offer Hope

1:3　I always pray for you.

1:4　I want to see you.

1:6　You are my chosen man.

1:7　The Spirit gives us power, love and a strong mind.

1:9　God has saved us through Christ.

1:10　We have everlasting life.

3:11　The Lord has rescued me from persecutions.

3:15　You know the truth in the Scriptures.

3:16　All Scripture is inspired by God.

3:16　It will teach, rebuke, correct and instruct.

5. Call for Commitment

4:1   I solemnly call on you.

4:2   I command you to preach, convince, reproach, encourage and teach.

4:9   Come to me soon.

6. Expect Results

4:11   Bring Mark with you.

4:13   Bring my coat, books and notebooks.

4:21   Try to come before winter.

4:22   God's grace is with you.

Now, let's break this outline down so that we can compare it against the PIER teaching. I have already given the *P*—there are six points. The *I* is always the easiest, because we all love to give instructions (just be sure the instructions are appropriate for the direction you take with the message). The *R* for reference has already been done—I have matched the Scripture to the six points and identified each verse. This means that there is only the *E* left for you to do to make this message your own. Your examples (or those of your pupils if you are doing this in a small-group setting) should be done on two levels: (1) What this means in the context of Paul and Timothy's relationship; and (2) What example this brings out in your life and the experiences of your audience.

When I work on a lesson like this, I take out six pieces of paper. As Marita has already instructed, on the top of each sheet I write the point, the *P*. Under it, I write brief instructions for that point, the *I*. Close to the bottom, I add the reference Scripture or other quotes, the *R*. This leaves me with the bulk of the space for examples, the *E*. I like to have an abundance of examples so that I can be free to vary them to fit the audience.

Teaching the Lesson

For me, these six pages become my working outline. By the time I'm ready to give the presentation, I will have the outline down to one or two pages.

My aim is to have no notes except the Scripture passages. Here is what I—and you—could do with this information to form it into a teaching.

1. Establish Need

Using 2 Timothy 3:1-5, I would use newspaper articles or magazine covers to show that, as in Paul's era, we are living in bad times. I would keep my examples as close to today's news as possible. The goal is to show that the Bible is as up to date as this week's problems, not some ancient history book.

2. Give Personal Testimony

The verses that emotionally grab me are "Everyone . . . has deserted me" (2 Tim. 1:15, *NIV*) and the verses that follow it under point 2, "Give Personal Testimony," in the Bible verse outline above. Paul was the best-known speaker of his time and people flocked to hear him. But when he was in jail, his following fell away. People who loved him then distanced themselves from him, just as the disciples did with Jesus when He experienced tough times. You could show how this illustrates flawed human nature. People are with you when you are somebody but then don't know you when you fall. Have you ever felt left out or deserted?

3. Present a Plan

This section is so rich on advice for any era that I can hardly take out one line. Can't you think of a time when you needed this counsel? I'm sure that if you think about your life experiences for even a moment, you will find amazing examples that would fit most of these verses. For me, I think back to a time when our CLASS staff went out to dinner and our attractive young waiter asked us what we did. When we told him, he backed up and hung his head a bit. Then he said, "I used to be a leader in our church." It was a line I knew well. "I was the leader of the teenage group and the kids really liked me," he continued. "What happened?" we asked. "They fired me," he said. "That's too bad. Why?" we couldn't help but ask. "I took the boys out for a beer after church," he said. As mothers, we all blanched at the thought of the youth leader taking our teens out for a beer. And I remembered the words of Paul: Avoid the passions of youth (see 1 Tim. 2:22) and keep control of yourself (see 4:5).

4. Offer Hope

"I constantly remember you in my prayers" (2 Tim. 1:3, *NIV*). When I told one sad lady in my Bible study that I had prayed for her that week, she burst into tears. "No one in my whole life has ever told me they prayed for me," she said.

Because I had given birth to two severely brain damaged sons, I claimed the next verse (see 1:7) when my daughter Lauren was pregnant with my first grandson. The doctors had said that my sons' brain damage stemmed from an unknown defect that was probably hereditary, and I was so concerned. *Could I live through this a third time?* I wondered. So I had friends pray through this verse: "The Spirit gives us love, power and a strong mind," praying that my grandson would have a sound mind.

He does—and my other two grandsons do also. What a blessing of God it is to have the verse you need appear before you at just the right time!

5. Call for Commitment

In 2 Timothy, Paul commands Timothy to preach and encourage his flock. He has already told him to stop whining and move into his calling: to be Paul's replacement in the ministry. I'm sure it took all the strength Paul had to emotionally pass his calling on to his young protégé. In the past, this challenge facing Paul didn't affect me personally. But now as I am in my later years and people ask, "How long are you going to keep this up?" I have a heart for Paul as he tries to be brave about his age and infirmities.

Recently, I had a debilitating bout of pneumonia. My son, Fred, came when I called, "Come to me soon" (see 4:9). Marita flew in to be with me in the hospital and slept on a cot in my room. "Come to me soon." When Marita had to leave, Lauren drove up to take me home. "Come to me soon." Those four words have emotional impact when we are in need, and I am blessed that my children all came to me soon.

6. Expect Results

Paul lets Timothy know that he has faith in him. "When you come," he tells Timothy, believing that he *will* come, "bring Mark with you, and my coat [I have few warm clothes here in the prison], books [there's no library here] and notebooks [I'd like to write just one more book]" (see 4:13). Paul adds, "And try to get here before winter [it's so cold here]. And, Timothy, may God's grace be with you" (see 4:21-22).

This year especially, I relate to Paul as he writes what turned out to be his last book. I've written three this year, and I have been asked to write an end-of-the-line book with my protégé, Emilie Barnes. Paul didn't know how long he'd be around, but he kept the faith even in adverse circumstances. I don't have his problems. I've never been in jail. I've always had a warm bed and enough food. I'm over my brief illness, and my faith endures. I'm looking forward to the future. Maybe I'll write a few more books.

Putting Your Best Speech Forward

MARITA LITTUAER

- -

Like anyone starting out in a new business, most beginning speakers feel a need to accept any speaking invitation that comes their way, whether or not it is the best fit for their style or skill level. They desire to simply get "out there," believing that once people hear them, the bookings will follow. However, it takes some experience to determine exactly what your style is—and to what types of groups you will be most comfortable speaking.

After speaking professionally for about 15 years, I discovered this the hard way. It had never occurred to me that I couldn't do everything. In fact, I can do a wide variety of speaking, but not every opportunity is the best fit for my message and style. Certain settings do not allow me to be my best. Would I want to accept an invitation for an event that is not my forte? I think not.

As a female Christian speaker, I was often asked to speak at women's retreats. However, I almost always left the retreat feeling as if both those in attendance and the organizers were not happy with me—that somehow I had not met their expectations. When I spoke at other events, I knew I had done a good job, I knew the organizers were happy, and I knew I had been the right speaker for that group. So, when I thought about retreats, I didn't think that my discomfort was because I was a poor speaker. I didn't know what it was—until I shared the platform at a retreat with another speaker friend of mine.

Marilyn Heavilin and I wanted to do some speaking together. Since it is more fun to travel with a friend and our styles and messages were very different, we felt that the two of us combined could meet just about everyone's needs. One of the events we spoke at together was a women's retreat. I shared the topics of my heart, and Marilyn shared hers.

As I watched the women at the retreat react to Marilyn's message, I suddenly realized why I never felt a peace following a women's retreat: I am not a retreat speaker. I had never heard anyone make a distinction between speaking at a workshop or seminar and speaking at a retreat. But now I knew there was one.

Marilyn has a moving personal testimony that touches people—often to the point of tears. Her topic attracts other women to confide in her. She talks with them, offers guidance and prays with them. Each of her messages builds on the other, bringing the audience to a spiritual place in which they find consolation at the foot of the cross. Sometimes, she has audience members write their burdens on a card and then drop them at the foot of the cross. When appropriate, the cards are burned, symbolizing the person's giving of his or her cares to Jesus. Marilyn's testimony, topics and personal touch create the expected retreat experience: People's emotions are touched, they feel close to God, and they make a commitment.

After that weekend with Marilyn, I came home and began to rework my promotional materials, removing the words "Retreat Speaker" from my list. I realized that my speaking abilities are best suited to seminars, workshops and one-day conferences. My style is humorous and dramatic. I do not have a moving personal testimony. No one cries when I speak. They leave motivated and equipped to improve their relationships with God, their family and their friends. I like to teach, offering practical step-by-step guidance. When I am finished, my audiences do not feel warm and fuzzy. They feel that they can do it—whatever "it" is.

Once I had made this self-discovery, I still had a few retreat commitments that I needed to fulfill. At one of those last retreats, an evaluation of my speaking removed any doubt that I might have had about who I am as a speaker. At the end of the retreat, the attendees had filled out evaluation forms, which the meeting planner had then gathered up. I was alone in my room packing up my remaining books when three attendees walked in with their forms in hand. They greeted, hugged and thanked me and, on the way out the door, left their evaluations at the designated location.

I looked over at the lime-green forms. They *beckoned* to me. I looked both ways to be sure no one else was in the room, and then read the comments on the forms. The first two women loved me. It was the third woman's comment that provided the confirmation of what I already knew: For the question about the speaker, she had written, "She was a seminar speaker, and I didn't come for a seminar." Wow! That was it. Although I felt wounded, I knew that she had hit the nail on the head. I was in the wrong place.

Since that time, I have had the opportunity to be a part of the Women of Virtue team, where I serve as one of three keynote speakers for a day-long conference. I have spoken for luncheons and numerous "ladies' nights out." I have taught at writers' conferences and business conventions. Each of these events has been a perfect fit for my message and style. One of my favorite events was an outreach event for professional women. They did not want an overt "salvation" message; rather, they wanted to provide something appropriate for businesswomen that would give them some practical tools for life in the marketplace and introduce them to Christian women. I spoke several times that day. It was a perfect fit.

I liken it to sailing. I am a sailor, though I do very little of it in New Mexico. When you are sailing, you can have the sails trimmed incorrectly and still have forward motion. But when everything lines up right—the breeze is strong, the sails are the perfect size for the conditions and they are trimmed perfectly for the wind—you can feel the boat "grab." You know this is what sailing is about. Speaking is like that. You can do well, even touch lives—that's forward motion. But when you are in a place that is a really good fit for you—perfectly trimmed—you know it and you say to yourself, "This is what I was born to do!"

It took me 15 years of public speaking to realize that not every speaker will be right for every event. So if you are a beginning speaker, don't be discouraged if you have to try out several different kinds of events before you determine which is your best fit. As you develop, you'll discover that you can't be all things to all people, and then you'll figure out what kind of speaker you are and where you belong! Once you find that out, you can focus your promotional materials for those types of events. You'll be happier. The meeting planner will be happier. The audience will be happier. You'll be putting your best speech forward!

CHAPTER 11

Speaking and Writing: Like a Hand in a Glove

MARITA LITTAUER

• •

I remember when I spoke at my first writers' conference. At the time, I was known more for my expertise in speaking than in writing, so was a bit nervous about being invited to speak at a writers' conference. Wanting to do a good job, I researched my topic well before arriving at the event. The week before I was to speak, I attended the annual Christian Booksellers Association convention (now IRCS). I spoke with many different publishers' representatives from both small and large companies and received some excellent advice.

The first evening of the writers' conference, I was introduced and asked to say a few words about the sessions I would be teaching: "Promoting Yourself as a Speaker and Author, from a Speech to a Book" and "Speaking to Promote Your Book"—both areas in which I have expertise. Because this was a writers' conference, I knew that many of the attendees were probably wondering why I had been invited to teach on public speaking. So, when I stepped up to the microphone to introduce my topics, I shared the following with them:

I just came from the Christian Booksellers Association convention, where I spoke to publishers both large and small. They all agreed—they would rather publish a less gifted writer who is marketable than an amazing writer who never intends to leave his or her computer. What this means is that if you are out there speaking, creating a demand for your message, publishers will be interested in you.

This is even truer today than it was those many years ago. The first question publishers now ask an aspiring writer is, "How often are you speaking?" or "How many books will you buy to sell at your events?" If you have the opportunity to meet with a publisher or send them a manuscript, you'll want to impress them with a list of the places where you are speaking. Hopefully, that list will include diverse groups nationwide.

While good writing *is* important, do not overlook the value of being marketable as a speaker. In your quest to get published, realize that speaking and writing fit together like a hand in a glove.

Speak First

I actually advise people to speak first and then write. When you speak first, you have the opportunity to test your material to determine the level of public interest.

I remember once having some new material that I thought was great. I envisioned giving seminars all over the country and writing a book on that subject. I did TV and radio interviews on the topic. Several times, I called groups and offered to give my seminar free so that I could try out the material. After that, however, no one ever called to invite me to give that particular series of presentations again. How grateful I am that I had not taken the time to write my messages into a book, find a publisher, get it published, and then find out that no one was really interested in the topic.

Speaking on the topic first also gives you the opportunity to refine your material and gather stories related to your message. Each time you present a new topic, be sure to use evaluation forms or comment cards to gather input from audience members. Ask them what parts of the program were the most helpful or meaningful. Inquire if there was an area on which they would have liked more time spent. (While this question is phrased awkwardly, it turns the negative of "What did I not cover well enough?" into a positive—"What do you want more of?") As you give the presentation again and again, you can continually adjust your speech to meet the needs of your audience.

When you reach a point in your speaking in which you are holding too much material for the given time frame, are continually getting great feedback, and have people asking if you have a book on that topic, you know that you are ready to write the book. If you have already polished and refined your material through speaking, writing the book will be merely a matter of gluing yourself to the keyboard. As you write, pretend that you have an audience that wants to hear everything you have to say on the subject. Tell every story. Include complete instructions.

Many people have the misconception that no one will want them to speak unless they are published. This couldn't be further from the truth. At CLASS, we represent more than 200 different Christian speakers. A rough estimate would be that only one third of those speakers are published. Yet many are very popular speakers.

To get started in public speaking—assuming that you already know how to speak and have a message that people want to hear (as outlined in the previous chapters)—begin by creating an information sheet. An information sheet is a one-page flyer (front and back, if needed) that contains your biographical information, a recent photo, your listing of available topics (with a short description of each message), quotes about your speaking (if you have them), and information on how to contact you. Assuming that you are speaking to a Christian audience, the biographical information should outline your testimony rather than merely list your professional accomplishments and education. Remember, the focus for this audience will be what God has done in your life.

Your topics should be appropriate for as broad a group of people as possible. For example, if you want to speak about surviving cancer, don't limit your speaking audience to victims of cancer and their families. Broaden your message to include issues of adversity. Everyone faces difficulties, and most of the experiences you had with cancer can be translated to a general audience. Your information sheet should include from 1 to 15 topics. Give each a catchy title and offer a few sentences to describe what each presentation includes. In addition, list the type of group for which that presentation is appropriate and how long the speech takes to deliver.

Promoting Yourself

Most Christians have a difficult time promoting themselves. It seems to go against their hard-won humility. At the CLASSeminar, I remind students of the children's song "This Little Light of Mine." If God has placed this message on your heart and you feel called to communicate it, do you want to hide it under a bushel? No! You want to let it shine. You have been called to share that message with others, so you want to let everyone know that you are available! I believe that we knock on doors and allow God to open them. We sow the seed and allow God to provide the increase.

> If God has placed a message on your heart and you feel called to communicate it, don't hide it under a bushel— let it shine!

Promotional materials not only allow you to share your message with the world, but they also give the meeting planner something with which to work. When you are in the beginning phases of your speaking career, you will most likely be speaking for smaller groups who do not have a full-time professional doing their meeting planning. Instead, you'll be interacting with nice people who offered to be in charge of that year's event. Typically, by the time these individuals figure out what they are doing, their term will be over and new people will be beginning the learning curve all over again.

These novice meeting planners will take the exact phrasing you put in your promotional materials and put it in their marketing efforts— their brochures and posters. So think about how you're going to focus your own materials. Think about the fact that people coming to your event are giving up their time and money to attend. Therefore, who is coming to speak is much more important to them. Before they decide to attend, they need to have some sense that the event is going to be worth their investment of time and money.

Can you begin to see why what you write in your promotional materials is important? What you write will not only help the meeting planner decide to invite you, but it will also impact whether or not people choose to come.

Designing Your Promotional Piece

Your information sheet should include your name in a large font across the top or side and a current photo, both of which should express your personality and style. Represent yourself accurately (no glamour shots!). Raelene Searle, Speaker Information Sheet Specialist for CLASServices, tells of a time when she had hired a speaker based on the speaker's promotional material. "When two women walked into the meeting room at the church, I couldn't tell which one was the speaker—neither looked like the picture on the speaker's information sheet."

If you are creating your first information sheet, you might want to use preprinted papers. These papers have colorful, decorative boarders or themes and provide a very cost-effective way to create an attractive piece. Select the one that fits you the best, and print the text using an ink-jet printer, laser printer or copier.

If you are going to design an entire piece (rather than using preprinted papers and simply adding text), I suggest that you involve a professional designer. When you visit the designer, the more you know what you want, the less it will cost you to create a look that accurately represents you. Know what kind of a look you want and have all of your text written and available in an electronic format *before* you visit the designer. Of course, figuring out what you want the overall feel of your promotional pieces to be can take months, so start by paying attention to your junk mail and any other printed pieces that come across your desk. Collect the ones with colors you like, fonts you are attracted to, and graphics that speak to you. Watch for a pattern. Once you have a sense of what you like, show friends and family members your selections. Ask them which styles, colors and fonts best represent you. Every correction you make after the piece is designed will cost you more money, so try to have your prototype as perfect as possible.

Writing Your Promotional Piece

When you write the text, remember that what you write is intended to help influence the meeting planner to hire you and the potential audience's decision to attend your session. Your promotional piece will need to consist of several sections that tell about you, your topic, your presentation, and the need that you are addressing by discussing the topic.

Biographical Information

First, you will need a section, usually on the front of the page, that tells about you. Because it is hard for people to write about themselves in glowing terms, I suggest that you ask three friends who are supportive of your ministry to describe you, your speaking ministry and your impact on an audience. Then take what they write (which will usually be much more flattering than what you'd write), pull out the elements from each one that you like the best, and then combine them. Your biographical information should be written in third person and should focus more on your testimony—what God has done in your life—than your education, job experience, marital status and children. While those personal elements are all positive and there is nothing wrong with including them, they are not what qualify you to be a speaker.

Presentation Synopsis

The second portion of your text should contain a brief synopsis of each of your presentations—including a catchy title. The speech title is as important as a book title. Do not give your presentation a title that is simply the topic, such as "Depression," "Time Management" and so on. Isn't "Beauty and the Beast" more intriguing than "Image"? Picture the pastor's sermon title that you see posted on a sign outside of a church. It's designed to make people want to attend. Your titles need to do that as well.

Topic Descriptions

After creating the title, you need to describe the talk. I suggest a three-part blurb. The first part should catch the reader's attention or create a need. This may be one sentence or several sentences. (Obviously if you have 15 speeches that you want included on your information sheet, you'll need to keep this part brief. If you only have 3 topics that you feel comfortable giving at this time, you have more room and therefore can elaborate more.) As I mentioned previously, one way to create a need is to start by asking a question that most everyone has experienced and can subconsciously respond to with a "yes." That makes them want to read on. Next, you need to address the content. What are you going to teach in your session? If you have a clear idea of what your outline will be, you might list it here. Again, this may be one sentence or several. The third part should address how people's lives and relationships will be improved after they hear you speak and apply what you have taught them.

As a part of your description for each topic, you should also include what type of audience the speech is geared toward and how long you need to present it. For example, this is what I have regarding audience and time for one of my most popular presentations, Personality Puzzle: "This session is excellent as a half- or full-day seminar and is appropriate for both church and business groups. Presentation time: 1 1/2 to 4 hours." By putting the timing needs up front, you help the organizer plan effectively.

You may also want to include in your topic description comments from others who have heard your presentation. This shows that you have been "out there"—that other people have heard you and like you! You might title this section "What others say about [insert topic]" and include short quotes from previous event planners. Put the statement in quotes and note the person's name and the state that person is from (unless they are all quotes from your own city or state). The more quotes you have from people outside of your home state, the better, as it demonstrates that you are not simply a home-town speaker. Other optional items to include after each quote would be the name of the church and event and the position held by the person giving the endorsement.

Contact Information

Finally, you need to include contact information. In today's world, I encourage people not to list their home address and phone number. There are too many crazy people in the world to put your family at risk by passing your home address out to strangers. Instead, use an office address or a Post Office Box address. Get a second phone line that is just for your speaking business or ministry, or use a designated cell phone. Be sure to include your website address—which ideally will be www.yourname.com! Even if you move and your physical address and phone number change, your website will remain the same.

There's nothing wrong with being a beginner—we all started somewhere—and isn't it better to underpromise and overdeliver?

Put each of these elements together to create an information sheet that represents your style, your experience, and your fee range. Remember, the design of your promotional materials will indicate your level of experience to the meeting planner and what your fee will be. Using preprinted papers will indicate that you are a beginner, while using high-quality glossy paper with a snappy design printed in full color will indicate that you have a lot of experience. Make sure that your promotional piece matches your level of experience. If you are a beginner with a high-end promotional piece and speak somewhere in which your skill doesn't reflect what your materials promise, the meeting planner and the attendees will be disappointed in you. There's nothing wrong with being a beginner—we all started somewhere—and isn't it better to underpromise and overdeliver? Let them be pleasantly surprised.

Making the Transition

Remember, speaking and writing fit together like a hand in a glove. While your information sheet is primarily about speaking and mainly for meeting planners, it can also be used to further your writing aspirations. It can be sent to publishers and can lead to writing contracts. My favorite example of this is from CLASS speaker Raelene Phillips, who writes:

After attending the CLASSeminar, I worked diligently on my information sheet. I had only spoken on a few topics, but I knew that I didn't have to have spoken on a topic to include it on my info sheet. So, in trying to fill up my sheet, I added a little blurb about how I could speak about my dog, Dixie. I knew that I could share spiritual lessons that I had learned from watching her, comparing her reactions to me as her master to how I respond to God as my master.

At CLASS, I learned to *always* include my information sheet with *anything* that I sent to *anyone* . . . from Christmas cards to letters to book proposals. I decided to send a book proposal to Evergreen Press, a publisher that had put together beautiful packets of information for us at CLASS, encouraging us to contact them and send in our proposals. When I sent my proposal to Evergreen Press, I included one of my information sheets.

Imagine my surprise when I received a phone call from Evergreen Press. The editor graciously thanked me for the proposal, but quickly told me they were not interested in the historical novel I had proposed. However, he said, "I see that you do a talk about your dog. Could that speech be turned into a book?"

My immediate thought was, "I've never even given the talk! What would I write?" But then I remembered Marita saying, "Any speech can become a book and any book can become a speech." So I replied, "Sure, I could do that. When would you like to see it?" The response was "Yesterday."

Less than four months later, I held in my hands the finished product, *Puppy in the Pulpit*. That was in July 2003, and the book is currently in its *fifth* printing. In 2005, Evergreen Press published my second book, *Birds in the Belfry*. I am thankful that I was taught how to put together a good information sheet. Without it, neither of my books would have ever happened!

So, follow Raelene's example: Once you have your information sheet, get it into the hands of people who might want to hire you. There are several ways to go about doing this. You can include it in your Christmas card along with a note telling your friends this is what you are doing now and that if their Bible study teacher needs someone to fill in, or their church needs a speaker, they should think of you. Ask your friends to pass your information sheet on to their pastor, women's ministry director or Bible study teacher.

You can ask your pastor to send a letter to all of his or her fellow pastors. Most pastors have friends all over the country with whom they went to seminary. They know the other pastors in their denomination and the local group of pastors who may be from different denominations. Offer to create a cover letter that will introduce yourself (be sure to allow your pastor to review it and make changes as necessary), print it out on church letterhead, address the envelopes, and pay for the postage yourself. By doing this, you will make it so easy for your pastor to help you that he will probably agree to do so. Letters from a pastor to his or her friends or fellow ministers will get opened, whereas the vast majority of letters you send to unknown pastors will end up in the trash.

Another way to generate speaking contacts is to check the local paper for upcoming events that feature speakers. If your topic would be appropriate for a secular audience, look in the business section (or wherever your local paper lists club and business meetings) for the listings of that week's events. If your topic is appropriate for a Christian audience, check in the religion section, usually included in the Saturday paper, for the events happening that week. If the listing mentions a speaker, you know that that group utilizes speakers! Track the listings for several weeks so that you can be aware of all the various groups and churches that hire speakers. Call the contact number in the listing. Ask for the name and number of the program chairperson, and then contact that person to let him or her know you are interested in speaking to their group. They will usually ask you to send them your "stuff"—your information sheet!

Whether you get the contacts through your own network of friends, your pastor or your own research, follow up on the materials that you send out. Tell people that you are calling to see if they have any questions or if they need any additional information about your speaking. Call just once or twice. Don't make a pest of yourself. This process will allow you to plant the seeds. If this is where God wants you, He will provide the increase—the bookings will begin to happen. As you speak and touch people's lives, you will get additional invitations to speak.

When you go to a speaking engagement, be sure to bring a selection of your books with you or books from authors whom you will be quoting. As you are speaking, mention your book as a part of your content, not as an advertisement. You might read a short section from your book. You might casually say that if attendees would like more information on this topic, it is in your book. At appropriate times, hold the book up once or twice during your presentation. Doing this lets your audience know that you do have a book available for purchase. Whether the book is yours or written by another author, you will usually sell 1 book for every 10 people in the audience.

Kathy Collard Miller learned this the hard way. At her first speaking engagement after her first book was released, 25 women were in attendance. She eagerly anticipated that they would each want a book (and most likely want one or two for their friends), so she brought 40 copies and set them all out on the table. She was discouraged and embarrassed when she actually sold only 2 copies! Now, as the author of more than 30 books, Kathy has a much more realistic expectation of what her audience will buy. However, she does find that the more books she has available on the book table, the more books the audience buys.

A sale of two books doesn't sound like that will make much difference, but as you speak more and more—and to larger and larger groups—the numbers will really add up. The more books you sell, the more people your work will be helping! Remember, if you have something worthy of speaking about, you have something worthy of writing about. What are you waiting for?

CHAPTER 12

Earning a Living Speaking

MARITA LITTAUER

• •

My last batch of promotional materials cost me nearly $3,000—and I need more, again. The biggest bill was more than $2,000 for new information sheets. A few months prior, I spent around $200 on the combination of a photography sitting and the purchase of selected photos. Then I spent $27 on 25 photo reprints with my name on the bottom to send out to groups who invite me to speak. I also spent almost $100 to purchase the festive paper I used to create flyers for a program I planned as a ministry for my church. Then there was the postage to send out the hundreds of announcements I made with that paper.

Why am I telling you this? Am I a bad shopper? Could I have found better prices? I've shopped around. Perhaps I could have saved a few dollars here or there, but I've learned that you truly do get what you pay for. I'm happy with both my product and its price. I mention this to emphasize the fact that as with any business, the speaking business has start-up costs, operating costs and advertising costs. Often, as Christians, we think that it's wrong to charge people for our time. We think that we should give freely as part of our ministry.

I used to be in a fellowship group for Christian speakers and writers. At one meeting, a speaker told us about a speaking engagement she had that required her to make a long drive to a church in the mountains, where she was to address a group of 20 women. No specified fee had been established, nor was there any agreement to have her travel expenses covered. At the conclusion of the event, the hostess gushed a thank-you and gave the speaker a plant, which was lacking even a pretty pot and appeared to have recently been ripped from the wilds surrounding the church.

While we were entertained by this vignette, the sad fact is that the speaker spent hours on the road getting to this event—not including her personal preparation, packing time, or the time of the actual engagement—and received no compensation (besides a plant). Our whole group encouraged this speaker to set some moderate fees for her time, both to compensate her and to improve the quality of the groups at which she speaks. However, she said that she was uncomfortable charging for her speaking because she sees what she does as a ministry.

I don't want to appear cruel or heartless. Ministry certainly is a part of this whole picture, but for those of you who are reading this and who either are, or hope to be, professional speakers and writers, my recent expenditures and my speaker friend's story illustrate that despite our desire to minister, there are costs involved.

Setting Fees

Is it possible to earn a living speaking? Not in the beginning. Most of us start out, like my speaker friend, doing the "freebies." We are always doing the "ministry" work. At CLASS, we call this beginning phase the PITS—"Putting In Time Speaking." We do this as we test the water. We need to see if there is an interest in what we have to say. It allows God to show us if this is where He wants us and if we are ready to be there. It also gives us time to perfect our material.

When God provides the increase and we receive more and more requests to speak, it's time to move on to the next level. Costs increase above the simple wear and tear on the car and the gas, groups start asking for pictures and biographical information, and even time off work or child care may be needed. At this stage, it is time to be compensated.

Although individual speakers need to set their fees at a level with which they are comfortable and which meet their needs, there are a few guidelines that they should follow.

Industry Standards

For the new, unknown speaker who hasn't published any books but who has "Put In Time" (what I call a "C" list speaker), I have found that a fee of between $200 and $300 for a single presentation, such as a luncheon or banquet, is normal and acceptable. For a multi-session engagement, such as a one-day seminar or weekend retreat, $300 to $600 is appropriate. While it may not seem right to charge a group $300 for a single presentation and then do a four or five session retreat for $600, that is how it is done—it's somewhat like a package deal!

I consider myself a mid-level speaker—a "B" list speaker. This group includes those of us who have quite a few years of speaking under our belts, have written some books, and have done a fair amount of TV and radio interviews. We are known but not so well-known that our presence on a given program will bring people from far and wide to hear us. For this group, I find fees of $800 to $1,000 for a single session and $2,000 to $2,500 for a weekend package are acceptable.

What I call the "A" list speakers are those whom we've all heard about. They've written countless books and made numerous media guest appearances. These speakers usually have several employees who answer calls, respond to letters, handle travel arrangements, and pack and ship books to each speaking engagement. This group would include people like my mother, Florence Littauer, Stormie Omartian, John Trent and Patsy Clairmont. Fees for speakers in this group would begin at $3,000 and go up from there.

Fees are always quoted "plus expenses," which means that any travel, food or lodging costs are over and above the quoted fee. At CLASS, if the event is within an hour's drive of the speaker's home and no overnight accommodations are needed, we do not add any travel costs. If the travel time is more than an hour, we add $.405 per mile. So, for a four-hour drive round-trip, we'd bill 240 miles. If air travel is needed, it is either booked by the sponsor or billed to the sponsor. Miscellaneous costs such as airport parking fees, shuttle fees or sky cap tips are usually absorbed by the speaker.

Per Person

Many beginning speakers find the "per person" method, in which the fee is based on a certain amount charged for each person attending, to be very helpful. This method also allows the meeting planner to budget properly. For a single-session presentation (such as a luncheon or banquet), I usually suggest a minimum fee of $2 per person. If the group expects to have 100 people in attendance, the speaker's fee would be $200. For a multi-session event (such as a seminar or retreat), I suggest $1 per person per talk. With 100 people in attendance at a retreat in which the speaker is expected to speak four times, he or she would receive a minimum of $400.

> When God provides the increase and we receive more and more requests to speak, it's time to move on to the next level.

Ruth Crow found a per-person approach was much easier for her when she was ready to graduate from free to fee. She writes:

When I was contacted by an acquaintance and asked to conduct a weekend retreat to speak four times on the Personalities, I was not prepared to discuss fees. I said that my fee was $10 per person to cover materials, plus expenses. I emphasized that this was only a *fee for materials,* because I did not want anything to prevent me from conducting the retreat.

The materials I used retailed for $10. The group included 28 women—all of whom seemed happy with the event—and they made donations to cover my expenses such as car expenses, printing costs for other handouts and so on. My costs for food and lodging for the weekend were covered by the Christian lodge where the event took place. My expenses were covered, and I felt that I was "Putting In Time Speaking."

About six months later, another event planner heard about one of my workshops and contacted me about conducting another retreat for 50 to 75 women. Because I knew that she was planning to call, I had time to pray and consider what fee to charge. When she called, I told her that it would be $20 per person, plus expenses. I kept it simple and did not discuss all the details. The $20 fee included $10 for materials and $2.50 per person per session for 4 sessions. When I quoted the $20 fee, it was an amount that she found perfectly acceptable.

A key to handling this difficult topic fairly is to ask the event planners what they want—number and length of sessions—before you quote an amount. I look forward to a time when I will not struggle with the topic of fees, but today I am consoled and given confidence by the guidelines that I learned. These guidelines have helped me understand what fee is appropriate and acceptable.

Although at CLASS we do not quote fees using this method for the speakers we represent, many speakers who are just starting to request compensation often feel more comfortable quoting a fee of $1 to $2 per person. This is fine. However, it doesn't motivate the sponsor to get a big crowd, as you will simply get paid based on the number of people in attendance. To avoid this, you may want to quote a per person fee based on a minimum number of people in attendance. If the actual attendees fall below your minimum number, the sponsor will still be responsible for the financial obligation.

Reduced Fees

I suggest that you develop a fee structure that is right for both your place in your career and your personal comfort level. To be fair, these fees should be quoted consistently. Of course, you may choose to accept a reduced fee on occasion. However, when you do this, be sure to let the sponsor know what your regular fee is, and then let them know that since they are your special friends (or whatever the reason) you are willing to reduce your fee to meet their budget. You will be treated better when you have a higher perceived value. In addition, you don't want word to get around that you are charging one group a higher fee than another!

Kathy Collard Miller has a good approach to this problem. When someone calls her and invites her to speak, she asks what the meeting planner's budget is. If the figure quoted is higher than her normal fee, she simply states, "That will be fine." If it is below her usual requested fee, she will respond with something like, "I usually request [her typical fee amount] . . . Do you think you might be able to increase your budget?" By doing this, she doesn't have a double standard but is still graciously able to accept the higher fee when it is offered.

Improving Your Income

Can you earn a living as a speaker? Not in the beginning. But you can begin to Put In Time, sow your seed, and at least get compensated for the true costs of being a speaker. Now, let's look beyond the dismal figures and see what you can do to improve the ratio.

Setting Up a Book Table

Most speakers (and especially those who are also authors) find that their highest percentage of income comes from the book or product sales that take place at their speaking engagements. My friend Marilyn Heavilin often speaks at places where she is paid minimally. She accepts the engagements on the grounds that she be allowed to sell her books. The book sales she receives are almost always double the fee she receives for speaking—and frequently triple.

If you are going to be a speaker and you hope to either earn a living as a speaker or supplement your regular income, you really need to sell books—even if you are not yet an author yourself! This doesn't mean that you stand in front of a group and hawk books. On the contrary, meeting planners would be quite unhappy with you if you came across as hustling books. By "making books available," however, you are truly doing the audience a favor! When book sales are handled correctly, everyone wins.

Obviously, if you are an author, you will bring your own books to your speaking engagements. However, to build a profitable book table, you will also need to carry product that complements your speaking topic. When Marilyn speaks on grief, she brings her books on loss in addition to a smaller number of books on the topic by other authors. Because the books and the audience are so well-matched, the sales are unusually high.

Evaluate your presentations by looking for places in which some support product might be appropriate. For example, I have a presentation that I frequently give called "Celebrate Being a Woman," based on my book *You've Got What It Takes*. In this talk, I mention three specific books that have been especially helpful to me in getting reacquainted with God. At the completion of the message, people often come up to me and ask where they can purchase those books. Because I know that the actual number of people who will actually go into a Christian bookstore after my talk to purchase those books is low, if I can offer the books for sale on-site, I do. When I reach the place in my presentation where I make reference to these books, I simply say something like, "This book was very helpful to me, and it may help you too. I have brought a few with me, because I find that many people ask for it." Then I move right on to the next point. I'm not pushing product, just making it available. By setting up a book table, I am doing the audience a favor and encouraging their spiritual and personal growth.

To start out, you may want to get books on consignment from your local Christian bookstore. This is a good way to test the waters. However, because most bookstores will not give a discount on consignment purchases, it will do little to help you reach your goal of increasing your income. Once you have tried some titles and found that they work for you, contact the publishers or a distributor directly. Ask about their discount schedule. In general, the more copies of a given title you buy, the better your discount will be. Also, inquire as to method of payment. Some publishers or distributors may be willing to open an account with you, while some may require payment in advance. Many now accept charge cards. Publishers want to sell books, and they will be happy to sell them to you, even though you are not a bookstore.

Offering Support Products

In addition to displaying your own books and others that support your presentation, you can also include other support product on your book table. Recordings of previous presentations are a logical addition. To add this avenue of income, start by allowing the sponsor to record you every time you speak—especially at those events that have a professional sound system all set up. You never know when all the factors will be working together correctly and you are at your best! It would be a shame not to have that event recorded.

By making books available to your audience, you are really doing them a favor. When book sales are handled correctly, everyone wins!

Collect all your "hot" recordings and take them to a duplicating service. If you don't know of one, ask your church if they will allow you to use their duplicating equipment. Depending on the size of the church, they may well allow you to come in as needed, make copies, and either pay them for the tapes or CDs at cost or not charge you at all if you bring your own blanks. Many churches are only too willing to help out people in their congregations meet this need. However, if your church doesn't have equipment—or is not as generous in letting you use it—they may be able to suggest someone local for you to work with. If none of those options work out, look in the Yellow Pages under "tape duplicating."

Other product options include selling greeting cards (if they tie in to your program), plaques, poetry, T-shirts or tests. In a message a friend of mine does on grief, she advises people on how to buy appropriate greeting cards for a grieving person. Since such cards are difficult to find, she carries a small selection of them on her book table. You can call these additional items "ministry support products."

The items that you purchase, such as books, will come with a suggested retail price, but for the "ministry support products," you may need to create your own price. Standard retail on a simple CD of speeches is $7 to $10. If it is nicely packaged with a full-color cover—which can be printed on your color printer—the price can range from $9 to $12. Other items are usually priced at the retail formula of your cost times two.

Getting the Word Out

Once you build your book table, you will need to let people know what you have available and how much it costs. Make signs for each product with the prices clearly indicated so that browsers feel comfortable and people who may be helping at your book table won't feel lost. Additionally, I suggest that you develop a book and DVD/CD/Audiocassette list with a brief description of each product together with its price, your name, and the ordering information. Make extra copies of the list to have available on your book table and print it on the back of your handouts.

Distribute the handouts to people as they arrive, or place them on the chairs earlier in the day, before attendees begin to trickle in. While the people are waiting for the program to start, they can review your product list and begin thinking about making purchases. If they can't buy everything they'd like on-site, your ordering information allows them to still take advantage of your books and other resources.

Whether you are speaking full-time, speaking as a ministry or just "putting in time," it is always rewarding to see people at your book table after a speaking engagement. It confirms that your message has hit home for your audience and that they want more.

Treat Your Speaking as a Business

If you really do hope to earn a living speaking and writing, you need to truly think of it as a business. Establish regular office hours and treat your job as a speaker as a regular 8 to 5 commitment. Protect yourself from becoming overcommitted to church and other volunteer opportunities.

Note that once money is involved, the government will call your ministry a business. Be sure to check with the appropriate state offices regarding sales tax collection and payment. Of course, you will need to pay income tax on all your earnings, whether they are in the form of speaking fees or product sales. With this increased income, you may need to begin making quarterly estimated tax payments. Consult your CPA or tax specialist for specific details on your personal financial status. If you do not have a CPA or tax specialist, check with people you may know who own small businesses and ask for the name of their CPA. It will be well worth paying for an hour of their time to get yourself set up correctly and avoid problems down the line.

The sale of books, recordings and ministry support products isn't limited to just the "big" authors who have written many books. It is vitally important for beginning speakers. Developing a book table will allow you to double or even triple your speaking income. Without product sales, it is difficult to truly earn a living as a speaker. But when you pair speaking and product sales—and add a little patience and perseverance—you *can* eventually earn a living speaking!

CHAPTER 13

Going Beyond the Book

MARITA LITTAUER

. . . .

Best-selling authors receive huge advances that make headlines. I pull out my contracts and check the numbers. Not even close.

I find that one of the key differences between inspirational writers and others is our motivation. No, we are not writing for the money—though we do hope to bring in enough to satisfy the IRS and offset our expenses. We may hope to be able to earn a living with our speaking and writing, but our ultimate goal is to get our message out there, to get our books in the hands of readers with the hope that our message will change their lives. We write from an inner influence. We believe that we have a calling that we must fulfill. Because we are altruistically motivated, most of us have difficulty doing effective marketing. It feels contradictory to humble hearts. Dayle Shockley, author of *Silver Linings*, says, "Marketing is the part of writing that most writers don't like. We would much rather our publisher do all the marketing for us, but as we know, that is wishful thinking."

But if we really think about it, if we are writing to fulfill a call and because we have a message that we feel compelled to share, don't we want to get it into as many people's hands as possible? Marketing is how to do that.

Over and over at the CLASSeminar, I find people struggling with the whole concept of self-promotion. I suggest, "You know that you are ready when you have something God has done in your life that you are so excited about that you can hardly keep your mouth shut." When you write from this inner drive, do you want the books to sit in your garage? No, they do not help anyone there. You want to get them into as many people's hands as possible.

While our publishers do their best to market our books, no one can convey our passion for the subject like we can! In addition, the publishers expect us to be active partners in promotion. If we sit back and wait for them to do something, but they are planning on our participation, the book may be pulled from print before it ever has a chance to develop momentum.

Spread the Word!

"I don't enjoy the whole marketing scene," admits Sharon Jaynes, CLASS graduate and author of *Being a Great Mom, Raising Great Kids*. "I have four books coming out within 10 months of each other, and I've had to learn how to be a little more aggressive with marketing. Publishers do not want to think that one of their writers is struggling with marketing. They are counting on us to do it." So how do we get out there and convey our conviction? What works? I suggest a three-pronged approach: speaking, book signings and media interviews.

Speaking

The first, and most effective, of the three prongs is speaking. Think about the last time that you heard a speaker who was also an author. When you arrived, there was probably a book table displayed at the back of the room. You probably noticed a few people slowly walk by, pick up a book or two, turn it over and set it down. However, after the speaker finished his or her presentation, the people were probably stacked two and three deep, eagerly pushing to purchase a copy. If you do a good job at a speaking engagement, people want more. They want to take your message home and share it with their friends. This translates into book sales! This is why publishers want to publish speakers!

Book Signings

The second prong is book signings. I find that many first-time authors have the misconceived idea that as soon as their book comes off the press, they will no longer be able to go to the grocery store without having people crowd around them asking for an autograph. The author pictures himself or herself at a book signing with their local Barnes and Noble—and a long line of people clamoring to get an autographed copy.

I remember my first book signing 22 years ago. I was one of three authors invited to help the owners of a local Christian bookstore celebrate their twentieth anniversary. They had been planning the extravaganza for months. They had made up flyers advertising the event and put one in every customer's bag at the checkout. They had mailed notices to everyone on their list. When the big day came, I was dressed and ready. I arrived at the bookstore expecting a line of people waiting for my colleagues and me. There were no lines.

Use a three-pronged approach to get out there and convey your convictions: speaking, book signings and media interviews.

There were no crowds—and not just upon my arrival, but throughout the day. One of the author's children had broken an arm. Because he had to take his child to the hospital, he was unable to attend. Of the handful of customers that came in that day, one person had come specifically to get an autographed book—and she was looking for the author who could not make it.

Unless your name is a household name, book signings will usually not be the most effective way to market your message. However, book signings can be beneficial to the overall process if you enter into it with a realistic mind-set and view it as one prong in the three-pronged approach. For one of my most recent books, I set up book signings with several local bookstores and scheduled each of the signings within a few days of each other. I then sent a press release to the local papers announcing the various events. Because of the book signings, the papers gave me coverage. One came to my office and wrote a big story about me and my writing. Without the announcement of the book signings, the papers may not have taken notice. In addition, each of the bookstores did a display of my book and included a notice about it in their advertising and newsletters.

At the first store, three people came to see me. One person came at the next store, and no one came at the third. I had to tell myself that all the people who did not come must have assumed that my book signing was already a big success without them. The stores had ordered my books for the signing—books that they now keep in stock because I am a local author. The advertising, promotion and displays would have never taken place if I had not committed those few hours to being in their stores.

Eva Marie Everson, author of *True Love: Engaging Stories of Real Life Proposals*, had a similar experience with a book signing at a big-name bookstore. She tells her story:

> I arrived beaming. When I walked in, the first thing I noticed was that there was no book-signing table draped in linen and sporting a vase of flowers . . . or anything! I found the manager. As soon as he saw me, he blanched. The books they had ordered had sold out, and they had forgotten to order more! Well, first I was thrilled. My book sold out! My book sold out! Then it hit me—they hadn't ordered more. Which meant that I was only a passing thought in their minds. Did that put me in my place or what! The fact that little ole Eva Marie was coming to their store wasn't the least bit important to them. However, two weeks later, using the same strategies in another big-name store, when I walked in I saw 50 books gracing the table and people already beginning to gather. The books sold out in no time!

Book signings are easy to arrange. Just go to your local bookstores with copies of your book in hand. Ask for the person who arranges book signings and introduce yourself. The staff is usually happy to set something up, as they are looking for ways to increase traffic in the store. Once you set a date, send news releases to all of the media in the area and send an announcement/invitation to everyone on your mailing list.

Radio and TV Interviews

The third prong in your book's promotion is radio and TV interviews, with radio being the easier of the two to arrange. There are thousands of programs in need of material (particularly talk shows that need guests). You are the answer to their problem. Like the book signing, the harsh reality is that they do not care who you are or that you wrote a book. They are looking for a topic that will interest their audience. Do not approach them with the attitude of, "Hey, look at me! You'll want to announce to the world that I have written this book" but rather, "I have expertise on this topic that is current and of interest to your audience."

Many years ago, when I was responsible for writing the promotional copy for all the books promoted through CLASServices's media publicity department, we were assigned to promote a novel dealing with the Puritans (yawn!). However, within that novel was a very interesting history of how the *King James Version* of the Bible became the standard of the English-speaking world. So I decided to write the promotional copy around that aspect of the book. When the author read the interview questions I had prepared for him, he said that they were not what the novel was about. I told him it didn't matter; it would get him interviews—which it did. But only the introductory material addressed the *King James* angle. Once the author got on the air, he was able to fully develop his real topic and introduce listeners to what the book was really about.

Look at your book. What is a hook that will interest the talk shows? It may not really be what the book is about, but it will get you on the air! Publicist Kim Garrison of CLASS Promotional Services claims that the most effective hooks are those that relate either to a current news story or to some sort of calendar event. Calendar hooks could be a holiday, like Mother's Day or Thanksgiving, or it could be a day that promotes a

> Look at your book. What is a hook that will interest the talk shows? It may not really be what the book is about, but it will get you on the air!

cause, like the Great American Smoke Out. It could even be a week or a month devoted to a particular cause, like Breast Cancer Awareness Month. The key to using such a hook successfully is to give the media enough advance notice to plan on using an interview with you. Magazines often need eight months' notice or more. Radio, TV and newspapers often need two to three months' notice. If you take the time to find and use a good calendar hook for your book, you will be in the running for the best publicity opportunities.

Media consultant Mark Mathis, author of *Feeding the Media Beast*, says that individuals in the media are often "underpaid, understaffed and under duress." With that in mind, authors who hope to get airtime on radio programs need to make the radio hosts' job easy. Do not expect them to actually read your book. Give them everything they need to do a good interview with you. Make sure that what you give them will ensure that the interview goes where you want it to go and cover the points you want to get in.

Realizing that radio hosts are interested in hot topics and not book promotion, write an introduction for them to use as they lead into the interview. The first paragraph should be a hook that makes the listener say, "Yes, I've been there. I need to hear this." A question is a good way to start it may be one, two or three sentences long. The second paragraph, which will need to be several sentences in length, should have some history on the subject, information on your qualifications, a summary of the book's content and a brief explanation of how it will help the reader.

Next, provide the radio hosts with a series of questions that will lead the interview along in a natural progression. Do not start with, "Why did you write this book?" Keep your topic and hook in mind. Be sure that the questions cannot be answered with a simple yes or no response. Your first questions should be introductory in nature, leading to the heart of your book while leaving the listener wanting more.

Once you have done the footwork, you are ready to contact the stations in your area to set up an interview. As an inspirational author, you should start with the Christian stations that you know have a talk show. If your topic is appropriate for the mass-media outlets, contact them as well. There are directories and services that can help you reach programs beyond your local area. You can do telephone interviews with programs around the country from the comfort of your home or office.

When you are on the air, keep in mind the key points you want to communicate. If the host asks a question that is not on your list or that takes you in a direction you do not want to go, steer the topic back to where you want it. Give your answer in a sound-bite format. Take a breath. If the host does not jump in, continue with a more complete answer. Be sure that you have information handy on how listeners can purchase a copy of your book—your ultimate goal!

Although you want to get your books into the hands of readers, don't just view interviews as a means to an end, that is, selling books. *Most* of the people you're talking to *won't* end up buying the book (unfortunately), so this is your *one* opportunity with them to communicate your message and make a difference in their lives. (Hopefully some will go buy the book, and receive even more from you.) Have a mind-set that goes beyond the commercial concerns. See the interviews as an end unto themselves, not just a means to an end. If you don't, you're not thinking about the listener.

> Have a mind-set that goes beyond the commercial concerns. See the interviews as an end unto themselves, not just a means to an end.

Kim Garrison suggests that you develop some sort of interactive feature on your website that will attract visitors. For example, you could post a quiz on your site that relates to your subject matter, and the quiz taker must enter his or her e-mail address in order to receive the results. This gives you a chance to interact with people as individuals and capture e-mail addresses so that you can invite newcomers to your newsletter list (a periodic e-newsletter is a must for ministries these days). The more relationships you build with people, the more likely it will be that they will purchase your book.

Sharon Jaynes, talking about marketing her inspirational book, says, "I've sent copies to contacts in other ministries. I've called bookstores. I've advertised it on the radio and called newspapers. Is it easy? Not yet. But, God has been so faithful. I think for me, I see it not as promoting myself, but as promoting the message God has given me."

Get Out There!

If God has given you a message, do you want to hide it under a bushel? No! Don't hide it. Get it out there! Doug explained it this way:

> One of the most powerful passages in the Bible for me is in 1 John 1: "We proclaim to you what we have seen and heard, so that you also may have fellowship with us. And our fellowship is with the Father and with his Son, Jesus Christ. We write this to make our joy complete" (vv. 3-4, *NIV*). I believe it is important—and imperative—that we do share our lives with others so that we will have fellowship with one another and with Christ. This is our calling. I am beginning to understand how sharing makes our joy complete. I look at you and your mother, and I see you living this passage. And I thank you, and I thank God for bringing you into my life.

A book is just the starting place. To get the message out and "make the joy complete," you need to get beyond the book. Book signings (as well as the coverage you get from them) and the media interviews will help you create name recognition. In turn, name recognition will make you more attractive as a speaker—another way to get the word out! I can assure you, if you try these three avenues for marketing yourself as a speaker and author—and that is where God wants you—you will get speaking invitations. If you do a good job, you will sell books and your message will reach the masses!

Dressing for the Platform

MARITA LITTAUER AND THE CLASS
TEAM OF IMAGE CONSULTANTS

. . . .

Your appearance is important because it reflects your sense of confidence (or lack of it) and gives you an air of credibility. As we previously mentioned, you never have a second chance to make a good first impression. People do look at your physical presence and make an assessment about you based on how you look. If your clothing is out-of-date, worn, dirty or poorly coordinated, this implies that the message may be the same: *You* are out-of-date and invalid.

Some people are naturally gifted speakers, and others have to work at it. Likewise, some people look great no matter what they wear, while others struggle with even the most basic outfits. However, those with little closet coordination can learn some basic principles that will transcend trends and give them the confidence they need to stand in front of an audience.

I developed some concepts many years ago when I was working as a professional color consultant. The majority of my clients were in the less coordinated category—the ones who needed help, and knew it. I would spend a couple hours with them, selecting the correct colors and advising them on how to use their colors. While it has been years since I did color consulting, I have always enjoyed teaching wardrobe coordination techniques. Additionally, we have a team of experts who assist our attendees at our various events with their stage presence. I've invited them to share their insights in this chapter as well:

- **Lauren Briggs**, my sister, is a part of the teaching team at our CLASSeminar. For years, she has done my mother's hair and makeup. She is a Mary Kay consultant and does "stage make-up" makeovers at the CLASSeminars for those interested in having a more appropriate stage image.

- **Jill Krieger Swanson** offers private coaching appointments at our Advanced CLASS for attendees who know their image needs some refinement. Jill is a professional image consultant and the author of *Simply Beautiful—Inside and Out.*

- **Tammy Bennett** has a professional background as a makeup artist in Hollywood and is the author of *Looking Good from the Inside Out.* Tammy works with us as our image consultant at Upper CLASS.

Each of us will be combining our expertise here to give you a few guidelines for dressing for the platform. (If you would like additional insights from any of these experts, please visit their websites: www.laurenbriggs.com, www.jillswanson.com and www.makeoverministries.org.) While fashion trends come and go, these guidelines will work year after year—for both men and women. If you choose to ignore these rules in favor of a trendy look, just remember to go back to them when that outfit is passé. Looking good can be a way of life that's always in season.

Dressing for Your Personality

My stage clothing has developed its own persona. I have learned that the audience responds to me best when I wear clothing that is dramatic, bold and different. People repeatedly make comments like, "That outfit is you!" They feel the clothing is me because my speaking style is dramatic and bold. I have learned that, for the stage, wearing clothing that fits you, your style, and your presentation is more important than the exact colors—though color is still important. Take your Personality into consideration as you shop.

Popular Sanguine

If you are a Popular Sanguine, look for bright colors, unique styles and clothing that has a costume feel. A *little* bit of sparkle and shine is a nice touch, but be careful not to over do it. Tammy suggests, "Stick with a solid-color shirt and pants or skirt, and finish the outfit with a funky jacket or blazer. One loud piece of clothing is enough for the stage, which means if you decide to wear a busy bottom, tone down the top." Wear larger earrings and necklaces that fit the theme of the outfit. Shoes should be colorful, matching the outfit. And consider adding a scarf to your ensemble, wearing it in a unique way—it's all about setting up your signature style.

Powerful Choleric

If you are a Powerful Choleric, shop for bright colors and simple, large prints in styles that boast clean lines. Jewelry should be bold and make a statement. Do not simply put on the same little gold chain with everything—which is the inclination of many Powerful Choleric women. Instead, use a wide gold choker or a dramatic pin. Keep both your clothing and jewelry clean and simple. The lines of the garment should skim your body, giving you a strong presence and a defined look. Remember, you want to make a statement, but because you are a strong speaker anyway, you must be careful not to overpower your audience with the use of wardrobe. Tammy states:

> As I've worked with a number of Powerful Choleric speakers, I've found that they have one common denominator when it comes to choosing an outfit: black and red—the power colors. Red by itself or black alone is fine, just don't put them together. A black suit with a light-colored blouse will take the edge off your Powerful Choleric nature.

Joyce Myers is a prime example. Early in her ministry, she wore intensely colored outfits that overshadowed her mission. Now, she has softened her appearance through the use of color, clothing and hairstyle, all of which help to downplay her powerful personality.

Guys, the same thing goes for you: Ties convey everything, and red means power. The rule of thumb is that only the boss wears red. If you notice, the President will wear a red tie when he wants to assert authority, but will typically wear a soft blue tie when he wants to make an emotional appeal to the nation.

Perfect Melancholy

If you are a Perfect Melancholy, aim for elegance and simplicity in traditional and classic styles. Be careful not to use exclusively the muted, classic colors from the beige family. I once observed a soft-spoken Perfect Melancholy totally dressed in beige from head to toe: beige hair, makeup, clothing and shoes neatly blended against a very beige wall. While she was perfectly put together and looked like she had just stepped out of an Ann Taylor advertisement, her lack of color was boring. Her message was deep and needed energy. The outfit could have worked better for her with the right touch of color framing her face.

Build on basic colors such as black, navy, gray, burgundy and royal blue; add red or yellow for a bit of drama. Antique jewelry will work well, as will basics such as pearls. Depending on your coloring, light/dark contrasting outfits can be a good choice. Many Perfect Melancholy women, especially if their topic and presentation style is emotional or sensitive, like a romantic or Victorian touch in their clothing.

Peaceful Phlegmatic

For the Peaceful Phlegmatic, an unstructured look with flowing fabrics is effective. Fabrics such as raw silk or a wrinkled gauze create the comfortable, relaxed feeling that fits the Peaceful Phlegmatic's presentation style. Colors in the earthy and muted shades will work well. Aim to create an artsy look with distinctive hand-crafted jewelry. Be careful, however, that your clothing looks fresh and coordinated. If you are a Peaceful Phlegmatic, you might want to take Tammy's advice:

> Find someone who can assist you in picking out a few good speaking outfits, preferably interchangeable pieces. For example, a jacket, dress slacks, skirt, blouses and accessories that mix and match with one another give you a simple, no-fail strategy for a put-together look. Remember, you do not need a lot of these stage outfits, as you'll usually speak for a different audience each time. However, be careful that you do not get so comfortable that you have the look of an unmade bed.

Regardless of your Personality, it is important to put extra effort into dressing for the platform. The things that work on the stage may well be things that you would never wear to the store or office, as they would be too much. But on the stage, in front of an audience, you want to have a look that sets you apart and lends dignity to your work.

Dressing for Your Body Type

When you are dressing for the stage, be sure that your clothes fit correctly. Look at an outfit that you are thinking about wearing and ask yourself whether it is tailored in such a way that it fits you in all the right places. Does it accentuate the positive and play down the negative? Does it flatter you? Did you buy it with your body shape in mind, or did you buy it because it looked great on the mannequin?

Most of us are not the size and shape of store mannequins, yet we often buy what's displayed on them and then wonder why it doesn't look the same on us. (The fact is, it's impossible for anyone to be the size and shape of a model mannequin and still support bodily organs—doesn't that make you feel better?) Take a few minutes to consider your body type so that you can buy clothes that are designed to work for you. Once you learn the shape of your body, you can flatter your figure by wearing the right clothing—and you'll always look your best!

Women

Tammy offers the following advice to help women determine their body type and what style complements it best:

- *Pear Shape.* If you have a pear-shaped body, your top is proportionally smaller than your bottom. In order to create visual balance, you need to accentuate your top half and downplay your bottom. Try this on for size: Wear a top with volume to it and a slim-fitting (not tight) skirt or pants. If you wear a jacket, make sure it hangs down to or below your widest area.

- *Rectangular Shape.* If you have a rectangular shape, your shoulders and hips are about the same width and you have a waistline that doesn't vary more than a few inches. To create dimension, you need to create the illusion of a tapered waistline. Try wearing a shirt tucked into a skirt or pants with a belted, low-rise waistband. Complete the look with a jacket that hangs below the waist.

- *Apple Shape.* The apple body shape is round and short-waisted, and the figure is not well-defined. If you have an apple-shaped body, the object is to move the eye away from the waistline by wearing a boxy jacket or blouse that hangs in a straight line from your shoulders to just below your bottom.

- *Hourglass Shape.* The hourglass figure is the most balanced of all body types. If you have an hourglass figure, you have wide shoulders, a defined bustline, a narrow waist (approximately 10 inches smaller that your bust and hips) and rounded hips. When dressing, your goal is to accentuate your waist. Wear solid-colored clothing with rounded shoulders and necklines designed to accentuate your natural curves. If you are short, stay away from prints that are large and overpowering.

- *Wedge Shape.* The wedge figure has an athletic, boyish look with broad shoulders that taper to a narrow waist and straight legs. If you are wedge-shaped, your best look will be made up of tailored and angular clothing that flatters your figure. Try a shirt tucked into a low-rise, soft-pleated bottom, and then finish your look with a wide belt.

Men

For the men reading this book, you also come in a variety of shapes and sizes, but your needs are not quite as vast as the women. When you're shopping for stage clothes (suits in particular), visit a quality store such as Nordstroms, where the salespeople are very helpful and will size you free of charge—whether or not you purchase anything. You will want to know your jacket size and cut—short, average, tall or athletic—so that you can purchase pieces that fit. In addition, you will need to decide whether to purchase pants with or without cuffs and pleats. Cuffs give you a more polished look. If you carry some extra pounds, pleats can make you look chubby.

Hosiery and Shoes

When you want to create a polished, put-together first impression, pay extra attention to hose and footwear. Although having shoes to match every outfit may sound extravagant, it can be the wise choice. If you have more outfits that match fuchsia shoes than you do outfits that go with a basic beige shoe, that shoe in fuchsia will be the more economical choice. You can look your best without spending the most!

When it comes to hosiery, play it safe. Unless colored hosiery is the height of fashion, stay with neutral tones. Even with the more natural shades, you can still make selections that will keep the feeling of the entire outfit intact. The natural shades include colors such as suntan, nude, beige, taupe, gray and coffee. If the total effect of the outfit is light, such as whites or pastels, use the lighter naturals such as nude or suntan. If the total look is more of a medium intensity, wear either suntan or taupe hose. If the look is darker, use coffee or gray or off-black—your choice would depend on whether your outfit is more brown (warm) or more gray (cool). If the outfit has warm tones such as off-rust or brown, wear the coffee hose. If the outfit has cool tones such as blue, purple or burgundy, use the taupe or gray shades.

When using natural-colored hose, the shoes and hose do not have to match, but you should select shoes that are in keeping with the overall look of the outfit. For example, if you only have two pairs of dress shoes, white and black, use the white shoes with outfits in which the primary effect is light, such as pastels and floral prints. Use the black shoes with darker outfits such as black, gray, navy, burgundy or purple. However, never wear medium or dark hose with white shoes. When in doubt, do as Jill suggests:

Choose a hosiery color that looks natural with your skin tone or one that is a shade darker. Wear these hose the next time you go shopping, and find a pair of shoes that match your nylon-clad legs. The closer the color match, the better. Not only will they coordinate with most of the skirts and dresses you own, they will make your legs look longer (and therefore thinner!). The neutral color of the shoes makes them an ideal choice if you travel and don't want to pack and carry several pairs of shoes.

Regardless of the color of the pantyhose, use sandalfoot hose when wearing open-toed shoes. "Sandalfoot" means that there are no obvious lines or changes of color in the toe area of the hose. Wearing reinforced toes with sandals or other open-toed shoes can ruin the look you have worked so hard to create. In general, I suggest avoiding sandals on the platform. When you are on a stage, your toes are often at eye-level. A closed toe will give you a more polished look.

In addition to the color, the right shoe styles are also important. Avoid wearing open-toed shoes or sandals with heavy clothes such as wools or corduroy. These thicker fabrics call for a sturdier, closed-toe shoe, such as a basic pump or even boots. In the same way, avoid wearing a clunky looking pump with lightweight, airy fabrics or styles. If you are limited to one style of shoe for all-year-round wear, a lighter looking pump—one with a more pointed toe and thinner heel of one to three inches—will be your best investment.

Undergarments

One area that is often overlooked in creating a smooth, put-together look is the area of undergarments: panties, bras and slips. I am amazed at how often I see a woman whose outfit is well put together but has a bra strap showing or a slip that is hanging out through the slit in her skirt. Inappropriate underwear is a big image wrecker! There is no way you can look your best with your underwear showing!

Be sure that you have a bra that fits you well and provides sufficient support. Also be mindful that you wear a bra with sufficient padding to prevent anything from showing through (this is extra important on stage and is a problem we frequently see at the CLASSeminar). You should have at least one low-cut bra in your lingerie wardrobe for blouses, sweaters or dresses that have lower necklines.

If you are wearing a blouse or sweater with a wide neckline such as a tank top or boat neck, you may have trouble with your bra straps showing. The most efficient way to avoid this is to purchase some thin ribbon. Cut the ribbon into a piece about one inch long and tack the middle of it down to the shoulder seam on the inside of the shirt. Then sew a snap on each end of the ribbon. Be sure to do this to both shoulder seams. When you put the top on, simply snap the little straps you have made around the bra strap. The top will stay in place and the bra straps will remain hidden.

Always have at least one bra that matches *your* skin tone. Bright or dark colored bras aren't the only visible colors—whites and cream shades will show through a white or light-colored blouse as well. Also, if you are being photographed, avoid bras made of materials with a shimmer or a shine to the finish. The flash in the camera is reflected by the shiny undergarments and clothing can appear transparent.

Although most of us eschew slips altogether in our daily life, they can still be important on the stage. If you wear skirts with varied lengths, you may need at least two different slips, a long one and a short one. A slip provides two services: First, it keeps your skirt from sticking to your hose. Second, it blocks light from showing through your skirt. For both of these reasons, be sure that your slip length and your skirt length are close to one another.

In addition, if you are wearing a skirt with a slit, be sure that the slit in the slip and the slit in the skirt line up correctly. Get what is called a petal, or tulip, slip. On these slips, the slit is tapered so that it is more open at the hemline than it is at the top, which creates a triangular-shaped opening. By comparison, regular slit slips don't really have an opening at all, just a slit.

As I observe women in airports, malls and other public places, I see that there is still a need to remind women about panty lines. If you are wearing a tight-fitting skirt or pair of slacks, there are two options. One is to wear pantyhose with no panties. Most pantyhose today are made with a cotton crotch and are designed to be worn as actual undergarments. The other option is to wear microfiber panties that are virtually invisible—or even a body shaper that goes from your waist to midthigh. This way, the edges of the panties do not cross your body at its fuller parts. Having wide lace edges on the panties will also help reduce panty lines.

Make sure that you don't wear something that you will need to adjust or fuss with while speaking. Some culprits might be a neckline that is too low or gapes open, a collar that folds down, a sweater or jacket that moves open, a slip that is too long, or a top that rides up.

Makeup and Jewelry

Whatever look you have worked to achieve with your clothing, carry that same quality into your makeup and accessories. For example, if you are wearing a beautiful summer dress with pastel flowers in a soft fabric, be sure your accessories complement that delicate look. Wear pearls or a lightweight gold necklace. Avoid heavy chains or necklaces with large medallions. Likewise, your makeup should be soft: pastel colors, frosted eye shadow and lipstick, lightly applied.

On the other hand, if you are wearing a trendy outfit with bright colors and bold prints, you'll want jewelry that is heavier and larger. Your makeup will need more color so that you don't look washed out. In all the makeovers Lauren has done at the CLASSeminar, her standard advice that she has to give over and over is: "When it comes to our makeup, what is appropriate for everyday activities is usually too minimal for speaking. Your makeup needs to be cranked up a few notches with bolder colors, more contrast and more drama."

Lauren states that the first phase of applying makeup is laying the foundation, or creating a blank canvas, onto which you will add the color, drama, contour and character to your face. Start with a clean and moisturized face, and then apply the following products:

- *Concealer.* The purpose of concealer is to cover minor imperfections, especially under the eyes. Apply concealer around the eye, both upper lid and below the eye, paying special attention to the inside skin between the eye and nose. The skin around the eyes is very thin—and makes it prone to dark circles. Create an owl-eye look that will be blended in later.

- *Foundation.* Again, the purpose of a foundation is to smooth out uneven color, minimize flaws and enhance your skin tone. Apply foundation using a sponge and do not wipe on your foundation. Instead, pat and press on for the best coverage. Blend into the concealer for a natural look.

- *Powder.* Once the concealer and foundation are applied, it is time to put on face powder. The purpose of face powder is to even out your base, set the finish and control shine. It will take away oily, or "hot," spots from your skin caused naturally or by lighting. Use a translucent loose powder. This should be patted on the entire face, including eyelids and under eyes.

Now that you have created a "blank canvas" on your face, you can begin to add back your color, contour and creativity.

- *Blush.* The purpose of blush is to create depth, accent your cheekbones, and add color and vitality to your face. Apply blush with a firm brush in an open C shape just under the cheekbone. Deposit the heaviest amount of color there and then blend in and upward with soft brush strokes. Do not bring the color all the way to your hairline or leave it in a little clown-like circle on your cheek.

- *Eyebrows.* For eyebrows, you want a full and natural look—not fuzzy worms over your eyes or pencil-thin brows. To add more definition to your eyebrows, if needed, lightly fill in with an eyebrow pencil in short strokes or fill with light brown eye shadow using an angled eye brush. If you have your eyebrows professionally waxed, always look at the eyebrows of the person doing the work. Is it a look you like? If not—run away!

- *Lips.* As a speaker, your lips are in constant motion and set off your beautiful smile. Choose a color that works with your skin tone and clothing but is bolder and brighter than you would normally choose. Use lip liner that is one or two shades darker than your lipstick. Lip liner is a frame for your lips and creates definition and drama. Apply just outside your natural lip line. To eliminate feathering or bleeding of lip color, use a lip outliner. An extended wear lip color or gloss is also a good option.

- *Eyes.* Once your eye area has been covered in concealer and then powdered, you are ready to apply color. I recommend using at least three colors. Base Color is a neutral color applied to the entire upper lid from the lashline to the brow. Highlighter is applied under the brow line for contrast and drama. The darkest color is applied in your crease for contour with the thickest use at the outside. Accent color is applied to the outer lower lid making a wedge from the outer corner. This color may also be applied along the lower lash line. Eyeliner is a must to accent and frame your actual eye. I never recommend using black, as it tends to be too harsh. On the top lid, apply the eyeliner above the lash line as far as your lashes extend. Do the same for your lower lid, but just under the lash line. The colors I like best are a soft sage green, a deep indigo blue, a subtle slate gray and a warm bronze. Mascara is used to lengthen and thicken your own lashes, again adding drama and definition. I have been very happy with the two-step mascaras that are newly available: The first step is a white primer that adds the length and thickness—which is especially good for people not used to using mascara—and the second step is the color.

Remember, all your makeup will look less vivid after an hour or so. Don't be startled if your makeup looks too strong. Step back and look at yourself in a mirror 12 feet away. That is the closest the audience will ever be when you are speaking!

Glasses

Try to avoid wearing eyeglasses, as they create a wall between you and your audience, and they will not be able to see the expression in your eyes. If you must use notes, print them in a font that is large enough for you to easily read. If you need to read a poem, put your glasses on just long enough to read the poem and then take them off. If you cannot avoid wearing glasses, choose a pair that works well with the shape of your face and matches your skin tone. Cool skin tones look best in silver or black and warm skin tones look best in gold or copper. Never wear "granny" or half glasses that make you look as if you are looking down your nose at your audience. Glasses—and all accessories—need to be currently "in." A little fashion sense is a good thing. When you stay on top of the trends, people think you are in-the-know on other issues as well.

A Few More Guidelines

Here are some commonsense reminders that we have collected over the years. While these may seem basic, trust me, each is included because we have seen the concepts violated in a speaking environment.

- Aim for a polished, put-together look. Make "hanger sets"—a *complete* outfit (jacket, shirt, skirt, belt, scarf and/or earrings) on one hanger—so that next time you have to grab your clothes and go, you won't have to play the "what should I wear" game. Put together a couple of business ensembles and a business-casual ensemble—or whatever you have chosen as your look, depending on your personal needs.
- Replace buttons if they aren't good quality. Plastic-looking buttons can cheapen even an expensive suit.
- Don't overdo your makeup or your hairstyle. Be consistent in the image you want to convey.
- Choose a hairstyle for its beauty and style rather than ease of maintenance. When standing up in front of others in a position of leadership, it is important that it appears as if you have invested the time and effort it takes to look good—which includes wearing your hair (your crowning glory) in a beautiful style!
- If you are short, it is better to wear a suit that has a jacket and skirt/slacks in the same color. Breaking up the color line tends to make you seem even shorter.
- Learn where the hemline of a jacket should hit your hips. Never stop a line at an obvious flaw in your body.
- Don't choose corduroys unless you are thin.
- When purchasing your wardrobe, remember you will be viewed

more from the waist up, so look for extra quality in blazers, jackets, blouses and sweaters.

- Before leaving home, view yourself in a mirror from all angles.
- Make sure your jewelry is not distracting. In most cases, less is more. Do not wear jewelry that dangles or jingles on stage. It will be a distraction to the audience.
- Well-manicured nails are a must if you talk with your hands—and don't forget to manicure your toes if you're planning on wearing open-toed shoes.
- Bathe, use deodorant, brush your teeth, floss and whiten your teeth if needed. Use mouthwash and carry breath mints. Avoid eating foods that cause gas or might unsettle your stomach.
- Conceal tattoos or body piercings, as they can be distracting.

Special Tips for Men

Clothes make the man, but the line, design and color of his suit are what make him look good in those clothes. According to Jill Krieger Swanson, a professional image consultant, the most important factor is knowing how to work with what you have.

Body Size

If you are tall or large, you will naturally appear more authoritative. Be aware that you can easily intimidate those with whom you come in contact. When interacting with people, try to wear muted colors (such as a medium gray or beige) and opt for a more textured (tweed or herringbone) fabric. If you are on the short side, you may need to incorporate a more commanding look. Wear pinstripe suits and strong contrasting colors (such as a navy suit and white dress shirt). Three-button jackets will add to the illusion of height, while cuffed pants will make you appear shorter. Keep clothing and accessories scaled to your size. Remember, you want a fitted look so that the clothing will not overpower you.

If you are heavyset, you will do best with dark suits and jackets with shoulder pads. Avoid multiple pleats in trousers and look for single-pleat slacks. Make certain that your jackets are comfortable and loose, even when buttoned up. If you are thin, you will do best with trouser legs that are straight rather than tapered. Cuffs are a good choice, as are pleats. Bulky jackets, sweaters and coats will fill out your body. Shoulder pads are a must!

Top 10 Tie Tips

A tie is a man's personal status symbol and reflects his credibility, competence and character. It can also make or break his total image. Choosing the appropriate tie will complete the look, not compete with it. The following are some basic tips to help you choose the perfect tie every time.

1. The fabric of the tie should complement the shirt and jacket texture. For example, a tweed jacket will warrant a tie made of heavy material, whereas a hard-finish fabric in a suit warrants a smooth-finish tie such as silk.
2. The color and/or print of the tie should be flattering to your face and add interest. Using colors like red, raspberry, rust or mauve will help give a healthy glow to your face.
3. A dark tie will give you a more authoritative air.
4. A light tie or one matched to the shirt is good for evening wear.
5. Tie tacks and clips give a dressy look, but must be of high quality.
6. Pocket handkerchiefs should complement the tie color but not match exactly—the same pattern would be too much of a good thing.
7. Save your black ties for formal occasions and funerals.
8. The width of the tie should correspond with the width of the lapel.
9. The length of the tie should fall somewhere between the top and middle of your belt buckle.
10. A well-knotted tie represents a classy dresser. Learn to tie one correctly.

Wearing anything other than a shirt and tie when speaking will take your look down to a more business-casual feel. Remember that when wearing turtlenecks, mock turtlenecks or a crew neck, the lower you go, the more casual will be your look. Be sure that the sweater or shirt you wear is made of a fine fabric (such as silk) and tight weave. It should fit well (again, skimming the body). This look is okay when you are trying to convey a more approachable persona; however, avoid it if you are talking about money matters or death or if you are assuming a leadership role among mature businesspeople.

Clothes That Talk

Know the language behind the fabrics and colors you are wearing. Often, they speak louder than the message you are trying to convey verbally. For instance:

- Pinstripes say that you are in control and distinguished.
- Leather can come across as aggressive to some, so wearing too much of it can make you appear intimidating and unapproachable.
- Tweeds are good if you need to get feedback from people. The texture and color-blend tends to make others feel more at ease around you.
- Strong contrasting colors worn together, such as black and white, can make you look authoritative or threatening. Wear with care!
- Soft colors combined (such as taupe pants and a lavender dress shirt) will make you appear more approachable and easy to talk to.
- Navy conveys authority without condescension, while gray conveys strength of character and a team-player mentality.

Leather Goods

Men can usually play it safe by having two pairs of dress shoes: one in black and one in dark brown. Also, a reversible brown/black belt is convenient. Quality is of utmost importance—your shoes and belt must be the best that you can afford. And don't forget that leather shoes and belts must be maintained, which means that you must break out the shoe polish and leather cleaner when necessary. Also, pay attention to the sole of the shoe. If you are wearing a refined, tailored suit, avoid thick soles and heavy leather. Save them for your casual wear.

Don't forget that it's always a wise investment to buy several pairs of the same brand and color of socks to match the shoes. Socks should match either the color of the shoes or the slacks.

Another shade option when it comes to leather goods is to work with your hair color. Gray hair is complemented by both black and charcoal. If you have red hair, you may want to choose a warm cordovan or rust for your next briefcase. If you have brown hair, leather jackets in browns will draw attention to your face. If you have blonde hair, you will find that tan and taupe tones create the best look.

A Few More Guidelines

Tammy offers the following additional helpful hints for men:

- Aim for professionalism in your overall appearance.
- Have your suit jacket professionally sized: short, average, tall or athletic cut. Professional tailoring is well worth the money.
- Professionally pressed shirts with collar stays look best. When you're looking for that polished look, wear a shirt with French cuffs and cuff links.
- Carry a slim wallet (no bulging in the rear).
- Wear a nice dress watch (no bulky sport watch).
- Use a professional pen.
- Invest in a classic-style overcoat that will serve you well for years.
- Avoid wearing extra jewelry other than your wedding ring and watch.
- Keep an updated hairstyle and never resort to a "comb-over."
- Avoid certain hair-coloring brands that may deposit a reddish tint on your hair and scream "hair color."

- Clean fingernails are a must, as most people use their hands while speaking.
- Keep all facial hair well-groomed. This includes mustache, beard, eyebrows, nose and ears.

Get It Together—So You Can Get Out There!

Remember, looking your best is not a matter of spending a lot of money but of knowing what to do with what you've got. By following the suggestions we've shared, you can be assured that you are making the right choices so that when you speak, your mind will be focused on the message and the needs of your audience. This way, you won't be constantly thinking about how you look or worrying that your attire might be distracting your audience, as was the case with one speaker at Beverly Dillow's church:

> As Women's Ministry Director, I had to find a last-minute speaker for a luncheon. I had previously received a call from a sister church a few miles away recommending a certain lady, and I had received other comments saying how good she was. So I called and invited her. However, when she arrived, I couldn't help but notice that her top didn't meet her pants and that her belly button was showing! I was disappointed, but didn't know how to handle the situation. When she was on the platform speaking, she was animated and used her hands while she spoke—and her top rose up higher each time. Needless to say, I missed out on what she was saying because I was so worried about her offending someone with her belly showing the entire time!

Take a few moments to put yourself together before leaving your home. By looking your best wherever you go, you are saying to others, "I care!" This kind of attitude builds others up and it shows them that you care about looking your best for them. When you are dressing for the platform, remember, you never have a second chance to make a good first impression!